Sto

LE CORBUSIER:
THE MACHINE AND THE
GRAND DESIGN

PLANNING AND CITIES

PLANNING AND CITIES

General Editor

GEORGE R. COLLINS, Columbia University

LE CORBUSIER:
THE MACHINE
AND THE GRAND DESIGN

NORMA EVENSON

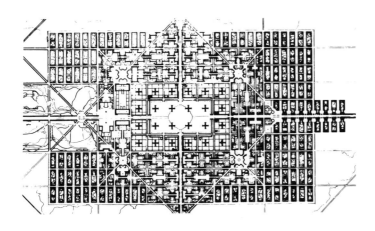

GEORGE BRAZILLER   NEW YORK

A note to the reader

In this book we have dated quotations by Le Corbusier as first published in French, although they may actually be taken from later English translations.

CONTENTS

1522944

GENERAL EDITOR'S PREFACE

The purpose of the present series of books on cities and planning is to make available to those who are concerned about present-day urban problems some information about the ways in which cities have formed or have been theoretically conceived in various historical periods and cultural areas. No period is more vital to our interests than the immediate past. Since about 1900 a number of architects have produced special images of the modern city that have considerably influenced the popular idea of the urban environment.

Of the leading modern architects, we associate Le Corbusier most vividly with urbanism. Although not a planner by training, Le Corbusier has probably done more than any other architect to direct attention of the younger generation to the importance of urban design. The combination of simplistic rationalism and lyrical writing style has given his easily visualized schemes an appeal to many—from the highly sophisticated contemporary theorist to the man in the street of an under-developed country.

Norma Evenson, whose book on Chandigarh is already a classic study of a metropolitan New Town, has ventured to write a biography of Le Corbusier as planner. His planning projects are well known, but the derivation and evolution of his urban and regional ideas have not, so far as we know, ever been the subject of a book-length study by anyone but himself.

It is our intention to provide a series of concise, illustrated volumes on individuals like Le Corbusier, which, with our books about different epochs and areas, will provide a complement to the encyclopedic survey books that exist on architectural city planning and urban history in general.

G.R.C.

A CONTEMPORARY CITY

According to Le Corbusier, when asked to prepare a town planning exhibit for the Salon d'Automne in Paris in 1922, he inquired, "What is town-planning?" and was told by the head of the section, "Well, it's a sort of street art—for shops, shop signs and so on; it includes such things as the glass knobs on the stair ramps of houses." Le Corbusier replied, "All right. I will do you a monumental fountain, and behind it I will put a town of 3 million inhabitants."[1]

The resulting exhibit, which included a 100-square-meter diorama titled "A Contemporary City for Three Million People," was greeted, in the designer's words, "with a sort of stupor; the shock of surprise caused rage in some quarters and enthusiasm in others."[2] Incorporating a rigidly geometric plan with a scheme of austerely uniform architecture, vast stretches of open space and a system of motor freeways, the proposed city appeared to some an audacious and compelling vision of a brave new world, and to others a frigid and megalomaniacally scaled negation of the familiar urban ambient.

The purpose of the scheme had been to establish a generalized solution to the problem of urban form; Le Corbusier claimed, "My object was not to overcome the existing state of things, but *by constructing a theoretically water-tight formula to arrive at the fundamental principles of modern town planning.*"[3] These principles, once correctly formulated, could then presumably be adapted to any specific urban case.

Le Corbusier was by profession an architect, already one of the leaders of the modern movement, and his approach to city planning was that of an urban designer. In the field of architecture he had sought to develop a standardized solution to the problem of the dwelling, believing that just as industry had produced standardized and presumably perfected object-types, a proper formulation of the problem of the dwelling could produce a standardized and universally applicable house-type. It was with this assumption that Le Corbusier coined his famous phrase, "a house is a machine for living," maintaining that a house should be designed to function with the same logic as a machine. With his design for the City for Three Million, Le Corbusier was extending this line of thought to produce a standardized city.

For most of his career Le Corbusier's relation to the planning establishment was that of an outsider. He held no official planning post, and was often at odds with authorities. Le Corbusier's influence on urban design, therefore, was largely indirect, self-generated, and maintained through his own initiative. Even though he was denied planning commissions for most of his lifetime, he may be credited with establishing one of the most pervasive urban images of our time—a conception of environment which, for better or worse, still underlies much contemporary design.

Although, superficially, the City for Three Million seemed sufficiently radical to alienate traditionalists, the plan synthesized many prevailing concepts of urban design, and incorporated existing trends in urban theory.

To Le Corbusier, as to many others, the modern city represented a problem to be solved. As he phrased it, "A town is a tool. Towns no longer fulfil this function. They are ineffectual; they use up our bodies; they thwart our souls. The lack of order to be found everywhere in them offends us; their degradation wounds our self-esteem and humiliates our sense of dignity. They are not worthy of the age; they are no longer worthy of us."[4]

Similar comments had been directed at the urban environment for almost a century, accompanying the transformations of the Industrial Revolution. From the nineteenth century onward, the cities of the Western world had been subject to unprecedented and uncontrolled expansion. As urban population grew, land use intensified and city boundaries sprawled, while industrial establishments contributed noise and pollution, combining with the growing blight of congested city slums to create an environmental squalor of overwhelming scale. Few municipalities had been equipped either in terms of administrative organization or technical skill to cope with the new civic burdens, and planning efforts were for the most part piecemeal and ineffectual in terms of the magnitude of the task.

The first major city to undertake large-scale redevelopment had been Paris in which, beginning in 1853, the Municipal Prefect, Baron Georges-Eugène Haussmann (1809–1891), having been granted virtually dictatorial powers by Napoleon III, was able to direct sweeping renovations. The most conspicuous results of his work were the new boulevards created by means of massive demolition and rebuilding, providing the city with a system of broad thoroughfares, together with a large volume of new construction. Haussmann's work indicated the scale of operations necessary for comprehensive results in the modern city, and in terms of both civic embellishment and technical improvements, Paris provided a model for many other municipalities. In spite of the outward success of the Parisian renovations, however, it was apparent that major urban problems were too deep-rooted and complex to be solved by upgraded utilities, improved circulation, and urban beautification.

The chronic problem of the rapidly expanding city lay in what seemed to be a continuous deterioration of the living environment. The poor were increasingly condemned to overcrowded, closely built tenements, while even in prosperous districts building congestion prompted Patrick Geddes (1854–1932), the British biologist and sociologist, to designate much upper-class housing as "super-slums." The phenomenal size of the modern city and the growing inaccessibility of the rural periphery produced an increasing desire to incorporate natural elements within the city, while a growing consciousness of the aesthetic and hygienic value of fresh air and sunlight prompted efforts to reduce building density. A distaste for living conditions in the central city, had, with the development of rail transport, led many to seek more salubrious suburban settlements, a trend serving both to extend the area of urban expansion and to place increasing burdens on the transportation system.

In the view of some, progressively inflated urban land values abetted by speculation and constant population pressures would render the large central city perpetually unable to provide a humane environment, and from the turn-of-the-century, the Garden City movement founded in England by Ebenezer Howard (1850–1928) sought to deflect the growth of urban population through a systematic program of decentralization based on the creation of self-sufficient new towns. Such towns would embody common ownership of land, be restricted in population, and physically limited in size through the employment of greenbelts. Although in theory Garden City planning did not presuppose any specific urban form, the movement came to be associated with a low-density, essentially picturesque, design.

While the frequently appalling image of the industrial city produced an understandable reaction in the small-town ideal of the Garden City supporters, as the twentieth century advanced, it inspired in others a romantic adulation of the new urban form and scale. The modern movement in architecture embodied an enthusiastic acceptance of the conditions of modern urban life, and a determination to employ all the resources of advanced technology to enable architecture to achieve a form suitable to the spirit of the modern age. Repudiating nostalgia for the past, the theorists of the modern movement reveled in a new mythology of modern man, conceived as a thoroughly adapted participant in an industrial urbanized society. The architect Henry van de Velde (1863–1957) chose to categorize man as "modern" or "premodern." Premodern man was characterized as a sentimental being seeking romantic illusion and addicted to meaningless thought patterns. Modern man, on the other hand, was seen as the product of an era of machine invention. Realistic and rational, "he eats, sleeps, works and amuses himself efficiently, sweeping aside irrelevant obstacles."[5]

Recognizing modern society as primarily urban-centered, architects began to envision architecture in terms of a new and comprehensively ordered urban ambient. This concern for the design of the total civic environment may be seen in a project exhibited in 1904 by the French architect Tony Garnier (1869–1948).[6] This scheme, which he called the Cité Industrielle, embodied a thoroughgoing presentation of an imaginary community occupying a functionally zoned site. The architectural design was characterized by a reliance on concrete, and the simplified geometric clarity of the building forms anticipated somewhat the stylistic manifestations of the International Style of the 1920's.

Le Corbusier had admired Garnier's scheme, observing that "one experiences here the beneficent results of order. Where order reigns, well-being begins."[7] He also found praiseworthy Garnier's employment of open space within the residential districts, pointing out that "hedges and fences would not be allowed. In this way the town could be traversed in every direction, quite independently of the streets, which there would be no need for a pedestrian to use. The town would really be like a great park."[8]

Garnier's urban conception may be linked to the nineteenth century humanitarian interest in model workers' communities, and to the growing concern for creating standards of hygienic and aesthetically agreeable civic design. His scheme emphasized that the realities of the modern world need not be incompatible with a measure of urban grace.

An even more emphatic and emotionally lyrical affirmation of the modern city soon appeared in the writings of the Italian Futurists, who eulogized the cult of modernism with a poetic imagery drawn from the forms of industrialism and the great metropolis. Among the first to hymn the joys of the motor car, the Futurists claimed that "The era of the great mechanised individuals has begun, and all the rest is Palaeontology."[9] "We must invent and rebuild *ex novo* our Modern city like an immense and tumultuous shipyard, active, mobile and everywhere dynamic, and the modern building like a gigantic machine.[10]

The Futurist conception of urban environment was embodied in a visionary project exhibited in 1914 by the architect Antonio Sant'Elia (1888–1916). Initiated by a competition design for a new railway station in Milan, the exhibition drawings presented fragments of an imaginary new metropolis incorporating high-rise building with elaborate multilevel systems of mechanized transport, the station complex combining rail and road transportation with an air terminal. The scheme was characterized by an emphasis on works of engineering, with bridges, viaducts, and motorways acquiring a seeming visual dominance over the works of the architect.

Le Corbusier's City for Three Million was in part a fusion of Futurist conceptions of speed, movement, and mechanization, with a Garden City emphasis on greenery and open space. As Le Corbusier described the plan, he stated, "The basic principles we must follow are these: 1. We must de-congest the centers of our cities. 2. We must augment their density. 3. We must increase the means of getting about. 4. We must increase parks and open spaces."[11] One could, by means of his plan, presumably both have one's cake and eat it; achieve the outdoor benefits of low-density living without sacrificing a high concentration of urban population. One could, moreover, have order, efficiency, and mechanization without foregoing poetic beauty in one's surroundings.

Like many practitioners of the modern movement, Le Corbusier adhered to what might be termed a romantic rationalism. In creating his scheme, he claimed, "I relied only on the sure paths of reason, and having absorbed the romanticism of the past, I felt able to give myself up to that of our own age, which I love."[12] To Le Corbusier the poetry of the city lay in its symbolic manifestation of the power of human action, of the ordering will of the human intellect, and although the plan incorporated natural elements, the geometric framework predominated.

Seeing the city as a perfect expression of man's ability to master his environment, Le Corbusier exulted: "A City! It is the grip of man on nature. It is a human operation directed against nature, a human organism both for protection and for work. It is a creation. Poetry also is a human act—the harmonious relationships between perceived images. All the poetry we find in nature is but the creation of our own spirit. A town is a mighty image which stirs our minds. Why should not the town be, even today, a source of poetry?"[13]

In terms of physical design, Le Corbusier's dominant predilection was classical. Although some architects of the modern movement liked to emphasize a total divorce from the past, Le Corbusier preferred to see the embodiment in modern forms of certain traditional values of scale and proportion. He wrote lyrically and perceptively of the drama of the Acropolis (*Fig. 1*), of the majesty of ancient Rome (*Fig. 2*), and admiringly of those who within the Renaissance tradition perpetuated the ordering principles of the classical world (*Fig. 4*). He loved the city of Istanbul, observing the serenity of its profile and finding in its many domes the "suave melody of very gentle forms."[14] He also praised the abundant use of greenery within this city.

The irregular contours and verticality of the Middle Ages he considered jarring, and complained, "A city can overwhelm us with its broken lines; the sky is torn by its ragged outline. Where shall we find repose?" To Le Corbusier, the choice was between "a state of barbarism and a state of classicism."[15] In spite of his advocacy of high-rise building, Le Corbusier found the jagged skyline of New York a wounding embodiment of "confusion, chaos and upheaval... beauty is concerned with quite different things; in the first place, it has order for its basis."[16]

The great emphasis which Le Corbusier placed on geometric ordering in his writings of the 1920's seems to have been in part a reaction against the picturesque aesthetic which had made considerable inroads into urban design, receiving impetus through interpreters of Camillo Sitte (1843–1903). A Viennese, he had published a book called *Der Städtebau*, containing an examination of the aesthetics of urban design. The book counteracted the mechanistic approach and insensitivity of scale seen in much nineteenth-century planning, basing illustrative examples on a varied historical range of civic art. Although Sitte had not been exclusively concerned with picturesque design, his analyses of the asymmetrical space enclosures, broken vistas, and intimate groupings characteristic of many medieval towns provided a justifying logic for nongeometric composition, and led some to regard him as essentially a romantic medievalist.

A particularly misleading emphasis on picturesque design had appeared in an influential French version of Sitte's book, and this evidently inspired Le Corbusier to employ denunciation of Sitte as a means of reinforcing his own views.[17] He reported that "I read Camillo Sitte, the Viennese writer, and was affected by his insidious pleas in the direction of the picturesque in town planning. Sitte's demonstrations were clever, his theories seemed adequate; they were based on the past, and in fact WERE the past, but a sentimental past on a small and pretty scale, like the little wayside flowers. His past was not that of the great periods, it was essentially one of compromise."[18] He concluded that Sitte's book was "a most wilful piece of work; a glorification of the curved line and a specious demonstration of its unrivalled beauties. Proof of this was advanced by the example of all the beautiful towns of the Middle Ages; the author confounded the picturesque with the conditions vital to the existence of the city."[19]

In what may have been an overreaction, Le Corbusier set out in a determined glorification of the straight line and the right angle. "I repeat that man, by reason of his very nature, practices order; that his actions and his thoughts are dictated by the straight line and the right angle, that the straight line is instinctive to him and that his mind apprehends it as a lofty objective."[20]

"Where the orthogonal is supreme, there we can read the height of a civilization. Cities can be seen emerging from the jumble of their streets, striving towards straight lines, and taking them as far as possible. When man begins to draw straight lines he bears witness that he has gained control of himself and that he has reached a condition of order. Culture is an orthogonal state of mind. Straight lines are not deliberately created. They are arrived at when man is strong enough, determined enough, sufficiently equipped and sufficiently enlightened to desire and to be able to trace straight lines." [21]

Le Corbusier saw the history of many European cities as a disordered accretion of accidental patterns, with curving streets following the "pack donkey's way." Man, by contrast, "walks in a straight line because he has a goal and knows where he is going." To Le Corbusier, whatever reasons may have promoted the nongeometric design of the past, "a modern city lives by the straight line, inevitably; for the construction of buildings, sewers and tunnels, highways, pavements. The circulation of traffic demands the straight line; it is the proper thing for the heart of a city. The curve is ruinous, difficult and dangerous; it is a paralyzing thing. The straight line enters into all human history, into all human aim, into every human act."[22]

To Le Corbusier, as to the theorists of the Renaissance, geometry was more than a matter of aesthetics; it was the reflection of natural order. "Geometry is the means, created by ourselves, whereby we perceive the external world and express the world within us. Geometry is the foundation. It is also the material basis on which we build those symbols which represent to us perfection and the divine."[23] Although he thus imbued his work with some of the ordering principles of academic design, Le Corbusier, like most modern architects, sought to disassociate himself from academicians, differentiating between those whom he felt had grasped the spirit and scale of classicism and those who merely repeated its forms (*Fig. 3*).

Within Paris, although he frequently poured scorn on academic classicism, Le Corbusier had unbounded admiration for works of the Renaissance and Baroque traditions, which he viewed as "magnificent attempts, rays of light amidst the barbaric stirring."[24] Such he considered the Place des Vosges built under Louis XIII, the Champs de Mars developed under Louis XV, and the Étoile and main roads leading to Paris designed under Napoleon. His particular respect, however, was reserved for the grand monarch Louis XIV, whose ambitious projects, including La Place Vendôme, Les Invalides, and the great Baroque palace city of Versailles exemplified this ruler's confident authority. In his writings, Le Corbusier paid "homage to a great town planner. This despot conceived immense projects and realized them. Over all the country his noble works still fill us with admiration. He was capable of saying, 'We wish it,' or 'Such is our pleasure.' "[25] In the same grand tradition Le Corbusier deemed "that magnificent legacy left by a monarch to his people: the work of Haussmann under Napoleon III."[26]

Le Corbusier continually chastised governmental authorities of his own time for their timidity, for their failure to act in the bold spirit which had created the great civic achievements of the past. Reverence for the past, he contended, did not consist of slavishly copying its forms or preserving its effects, but in grasping the essence of a tradition of far-reaching action and ordered accomplishment. Needless to say, he considered his own civic schemes a perfect embodiment of this tradition.

A CITY FOR THREE MILLION PEOPLE

The plan which Le Corbusier produced for the City for Three Million consisted of a rectangle containing two cross-axial major streets focusing on the center (*Figs. 5–6, 8*). In its essential geometric outlines the plan was rooted in one of the oldest traditions of urban design, the cross being perhaps the most ancient intuitive gesture by which mankind takes possession of a space, and it is believed that the oldest symbolic representation of a city is an Egyptian hieroglyph comprising a cross within a circle. The design contained elements of the traditional Roman plan based on the military encampment, and resembled as well the ritually conceived pattern of ancient Indian towns. In the Roman town the crossing of the principal streets marked the site of the forum; in India, the auspicious meeting place of the elders and quarters of the highest caste. In the City for Three Million the center provided the commercial district—a complex of twenty-four identical cruciform skyscrapers which would "contain the city's brains, the brains of the whole nation [*Figs. 7, 9*]. They stand for all the careful working out and organization on which the general activity is based. Everything is concentrated in them: apparatus for abolishing time and space, telephones, cables and wireless; the banks and business affairs and the control of industry; finance, commerce, specialization."[27]

To the left of the business district would lie a civic and cultural center, beyond which would extend a rectilinear, but picturesquely landscaped park (*Fig. 9*). The major street network would embody, in addition to the central cross axis, a large-scale grid and diagonal pattern relating to regional routes, while a smaller grid would define the residential superblocks surrounding the center. Within the residential districts, apartment housing presented a dual configuration, either defining the perimeter of a superblock or following an independent pattern of setbacks (*redents*) within areas of greenery (*Fig. 10*). The industrial district would be sited outside the city and separated from it by a greenbelt.

Although in the design presentation of the City for Three Million Le Corbusier concentrated his efforts on a portrayal of the central area, the total urban scheme incorporated a system of incorrectly termed "Garden Cities" sited beyond the surrounding greenbelt. Although the Garden City concept had been based on the idea of self-contained communities providing both residence and employment, such towns could theoretically develop into a system of satellites in which a larger center might furnish certain services not found in the outlying towns. The City for Three Million was not a true satellite system, as defined by Ebenezer Howard, however, for the Garden Cities would serve only as dormitory suburbs for workers in both the central city and the industrial area, and of the three million people for whom the project was designed, over two million would live in the Garden Cities. (It may be noted that Le Corbusier tended to use the term "Garden City" rather loosely, frequently misusing it to describe what were in fact residential suburbs.[28])

By and large Le Corbusier was unsympathetic to the suburban ideal of the single family house, pointing out that such housing was wasteful of roads and utilities, encouraged urban sprawl, and through its extensive land coverage, succeeded in negating the virtues of seclusion and peaceful rural atmosphere which its inhabitants had initially sought. Repeatedly in his writings Le Corbusier would contrast the pattern of land coverage achieved through individual houses on small plots with the building pattern which he himself favored, that of large apartment blocks widely spaced in landscaped areas. The advantage of this, he never tired of stressing, lay in a greater economy of circulation and services, the provision of large park and sport facilities, and also in the creation of greater privacy and vista for individual dwelling units.

Part of Le Corbusier's opposition to the Garden City concept, as well as the suburban movement, lay in his conviction that it deflected attention from what he deemed the primary problem in city planning: renovating and revitalizing the central city. Without a thoroughgoing renewal of the city center, he felt that efforts to improve outlying areas were irrelevant.

In terms of population, Le Corbusier envisioned the center of the city complex as inhabited primarily by the administrative and intellectual elite. "As the seat of power (in the widest meaning of the word; for in it there come together princes of affairs, captains of industry and finance, political leaders, great scientists, teachers, thinkers, the spokesmen of the human soul, painters, poets and musicians), the city draws every ambition to itself: it is clothed in a dazzling mirage of unimaginable beauty; the people swarm into it. Great men and our leaders install themselves in the city's centre.... So a classification of city dwellers would give us three main divisions of population: the citizens who live in the city; the workers whose lives are passed half in the centre and half in the garden cities, and the great masses of workers who spend their lives between suburban factories and garden cities."[29]

Within the central portion of the city, the architectural components were simplified to two major building types, the centrally zoned sixty-story cruciform skyscrapers with indented glass walls, which contained the business and administrative activities of the city, and twelve-story apartment houses occupying the surrounding urban area (*Fig. 10*). Defending his scheme against possible charges of monotony, Le Corbusier cited an axiom of the Abbé Laugier advocating "uniformity in detail,"[30] arguing that the urban design of all great periods had been marked by architectural unity. "Everywhere, before the disturbing influences of the nineteenth century, men's houses were boxes of the same nature.... *There was a universal standard and complete uniformity in detail.* Under such conditions the mind is calm."[31]

Le Corbusier saw no desirability in mixed-use areas, determining that, "Family life... will be definitely banished from the centre of our city. It seems most probable, as things are, that the skyscraper cannot adequately provide for family life; for its internal economy demands so elaborate a system that if one of these structures is to pay, only business can afford the cost."[32]

For the apartment housing, two building types were developed (*Fig. 11*), one, projected for moderate-cost dwellings, extended around the superblock periphery to enclose a large central garden, while the other, intended for more luxurious flats, embodied a continuous slab sited within landscaped grounds, and creating a linear pattern of setbacks separated from, but overlaying, the street grid. The apartment units, which Le Corbusier called "freehold maisonettes," were related to a prototypical standardized dwelling termed the "Citrohan house" which Le Corbusier exhibited at the Salon d'Automne in 1922.[33] Each apartment was designed as a two-story unit containing a double-height living room and adjoining covered terrace (*Figs. 13–14*). Describing this housing, Le Corbusier observed, "The 'freehold maisonettes' [*Immeubles-Villas*] represent a new dwelling formula for the large city. Each apartment is, in reality, a little house with a garden, situated it matters not how high above the street"[34] (*Figs. 12, 15*).

Considering the family as a somewhat flexible unit, whose domestic needs would vary through time, Le Corbusier was prophetic in viewing the modern city dweller as essentially a nomad having increasingly fewer domestic possessions, and requiring more built-in equipment. Describing his conception of the dwelling unit, the architect stated, "We must never, in our studies, lose sight of the purely human 'cell,' the cell which responds most perfectly to our physiological and sentimental needs. We must arrive at the 'house-machine,' which must be both practical and emotionally satisfying and designed for a succession of tenants. The idea of the 'old home' disappears, and with it local architecture, etc., for labour will shift about as needed, and must be ready to move, *bag and baggage*."[35]

Le Corbusier saw his city as one which liberated the individual from many of the complications of domestic management, and, foreseeing the disappearance of the domestic servant, sought to include a complete catering and housekeeping service within each apartment building. He felt that his civic conception, by providing for greater ease and convenience in daily activities, would enable all inhabitants to enjoy a more abundant leisure. Specific provisions for leisure activities within the residential districts, however, seemed almost obsessively centered on athletic facilities. Although the apartment houses would be surrounded by tennis courts, swimming pools, and soccer fields, and rooftops would provide sunbathing areas and running tracks, cafés, theaters, libraries, and shops were notably absent. Within the superblock areas it would appear relatively easy to play a game of tennis, but impossible to buy a glass of wine or a spool of thread.

Of perhaps greater importance in the development of the plan, in the architect's view, was the system of motor roads embodying the elimination of what he termed the "corridor street," the traditional city street lined with buildings, and clogged with slow-moving, frequently halting motor traffic. Claiming that "a city made for speed is made for success," Le Corbusier sought a total separation of motor freeways from building lines and pedestrian ways. In order to ensure the rapid movement of wheeled traffic, the texture of the block pattern was expanded into a grid of superblocks 400 x 600 meters in area, with secondary streets occuring at 200-meter intervals. Motor access to the apartment blocks would lead to parking terminals near the entrances, while pedestrian circulation paths would cut through the landscaped spaces, passing underneath the buildings which would be raised on pilotis to free the ground area. As Le Corbusier projected his plan, the amount of ground built over would be 15 percent, leaving 85 percent as open space, and with this achieving a population density of 120 persons per acre.

In addition to the motor freeways, the city would be served by a subway and an underground commuter rail system linking the "Garden Cities" to the center. At the center of the city, flanked by four skyscrapers would be a multilevel transportation complex (*Fig. 7*). The upper level would consist of a raised platform serving as a landing field for aircraft— a similar conception having appeared earlier in Sant'Elia's Futurist scheme for the Città Nuova.

The image of planes landing in the center of the city obviously had considerable appeal for Le Corbusier, who even ventured, "who knows whether soon it will not be equally possible for them to land on the roofs of the skyscrapers, from thence without loss of time to link up with the provinces and other countries. For the moment," he admitted, "the airport allowed for in the centre is a station for air-taxis connecting up with the aerodrome in the protected zone. Means of landing are not yet sufficiently perfect to allow the large transcontinental airplane to make its way safely to the heart of the city."[36]

Below the airport would be a mezzanine level for rapid motor traffic while slower traffic would circulate at ground level, at which point would be access to railway lines and booking offices. At the first subterranean level would be the subway lines, below which would be the local and suburban railways, while at a still lower level would be the main railway lines. Each of the skyscrapers would contain a subway station.

To Le Corbusier the City for Three Million not only solved all major urban problems of housing and transport, but combined man-made order with natural landscape to create an urban environment of unrivaled beauty. Having proclaimed that "the materials of city planning are sky, space, trees, steel and cement, in this order and in this hierarchy," he had created a city of sun-drenched open texture, swept clear of all disorder. His descriptions of the city rhapsodized the joys of rapid driving on the motor freeways, the perception of "immensity of space," of "vast architectural perspectives," with "the sky everywhere, as far as the eye can see."[37] The uniform facades of the dwellings would "form a sort of grill or trellis against which the trees will display themselves to advantage,"[38] while the skyscrapers would "raise immense geometrical facades all of glass, and in them is reflected the blue glory of the sky. An overwhelming sensation. Immense but radiant prisms.... The traveller in his airplane, arriving from Constantinople, or perhaps Peking, suddenly sees appearing through the wavering lines of rivers and patches of forests that clear imprint which marks a city which has grown in accordance with the spirit of man: the mark of the human brain at work. As twilight falls the glass skyscrapers seem to flame."[39]

Although the romanticism of the city was somewhat akin in spirit to that of the Futurists, Le Corbusier was at pains to disassociate himself from them and their fevered vision of a world to come. "This," he maintained, "is no dangerous Futurism, a sort of literary dynamite flung violently at the spectator."[40] "It bores me more than I can say to describe, like some minor prophet, this future City of the Blest. It makes me imagine I have become a Futurist, a sensation I do not at all appreciate. I feel as though I were leaving on one side the crude realities of existence for the pleasures of automatic lucubrations."[41] He insisted that he had designed no city of the future, but a city of the present; that it was for contemporary society and contemporary technology that he had conceived the scheme. The Futurists, moreover, adhered to a conception of mechanization stressing the rapid obsolescence of the physical environment, while Le Corbusier, with his inherent sense of tradition claimed, "It is the city's business to make itself permanent, and this depends on considerations other than those of calculation. It is only Architecture which can give all the things which go beyond calculation."[42]

As an urban image, the City for Three Million seemed to hover somewhere between dream and reality, but was perhaps more appealing as a dream. The scheme embodied an oversimplification of urban life and function, appearing to some critics as a formal diagram neglectful of many of the factors essential to urban vitality. As Lewis Mumford was later to write of Le Corbusier," he paid no more attention to the nature of the city and to the orderly arrangements of its constantly proliferating groups, societies, clubs, organizations, institutions, than did the real estate broker or the municipal engineer. In short, he embraced every feature of the contemporary city except its essential social and civic character.... Le Corbusier wiped out the complex tissue of a thousand little and not so little urban activities that cannot be economically placed in tall structures or function efficiently except at points where they are encountered at street level and utilized by a multitude of people going about their business at all times of the day.

"The extravagant heights of Le Corbusier's skyscrapers had no reason for existence apart from the fact that they had become technological possibilities; the open spaces in his central areas had no reason for existence either, since on the scale he imagined, there was no motive during the business day for pedestrian circulation in the office quarter. By mating the utilitarian and financial image of the skyscraper city to the romantic image of the organic environment, Le Corbusier had in fact produced a sterile hybrid."[43]

If many observers found the City for Three Million a frigid and inhumanly scaled ambient, inimical to social contact, the reason lay partly in the Olympian formality of the designer's presentation which embodied a god's-eye view of the large-scale visual aspects, but neglected to deal convincingly with small-scale function. It may be noted that the plan was intended to incorporate within the landscaped spaces in the center of the city, a network of low-rise, three-story buildings fronting on boulevards and pedestrian ways, and containing shops and cafés. "The street," Le Corbusier pointed out, "would thus be reorganized on a human scale. In this City of Skyscrapers we should, in fact, be able to restore just that very scale which is really in conformity with our own dimensions: the one-storeyed house.

"And so my scheme, which at first glance might seem to warrant a certain fear and dislike, brings us back to something we have had to forego with regret in towns of the nineteenth century: architecture to our own scale.

"We are fond of the crowd and the crush because we are human beings and like to live in groups. In such a town as I have outlined, with a denser population than that of any existing cities, there would be ample provision and opportunity for close human contact."[44]

In spite of such reassurance, relatively few viewers seemed able to identify favorably with the conception of urban life implied in the City for Three Million. A contemporary French architectural journal commiserated with the imaginary inhabitants of such a city, "Poor creatures! What will they become in the midst of all this dreadful speed, this organization, this terrible uniformity?...here is enough to disgust one for ever with 'standardization' and to make one long for 'disorder.'"[45]

THE VOISIN PLAN

For those who had been unnerved by the scale of the City for Three Million, Le Corbusier soon produced an even more alarming exhibition project, a scheme which would apply similar principles to a redevelopment of the center of Paris. Convinced that the motor car had both killed and would save the city, Le Corbusier had approached several automobile manufacturers with a view to obtaining sponsorship for the Esprit Nouveau pavilion at the Paris International Exhibition of Decorative Art in 1925. Voisin had responded favorably, and was subsequently honored by having the exhibition plan named for him.

The proposed scheme would involve demolition and reconstruction to create a new commercial center and residential district: the commercial center designed to occupy 600 acres of a "particularly antiquated and unhealthy part of Paris, i.e. from the Place de la République to the Rue du Louvre, and from the Gare de l'Est to the Rue de Rivoli," while the residential district would extend from the Rue des Pyramides to the circus on the Champs Élysées, and from the Gare Saint-Lazare to the Rue de Rivoli, a district which the architect described as "for the most part overcrowded, and covered with middle-class houses now used as offices"[46] (*Figs. 16–17*). Incorporated in the scheme would be a new motor freeway creating an east-west axis from Vincennes to

Levaillois-Perret, and intended to draw traffic away from the Champs Élysées (*Figs. 23–24*). Within the area of demolition which comprised much of the historic center of Paris, Le Corbusier intended to leave selected structures untouched, enabling one to find "still standing among the masses of foliage of the new parks, certain historical monuments, arcades, doorways, carefully preserved because they are pages out of history or works of art."[47]

Far from destroying the monuments of the past through his massive demolitions, Le Corbusier claimed to be giving them a more peaceful setting, maintaining that "the past has lost something of its fragrance, for its enforced mingling with the life of today has set it in a false environment. My dream is to see the Place de la Concorde empty once more, silent and lonely, and the Champs Élysées a quiet place to walk in."[48]

Although the new scheme created a sharp and coarse contrast with the existing fabric of Paris, juxtaposing within the low-rise texture of the city the sudden looming presence of 245-meter skyscrapers, Le Corbusier saw no disharmony between his scheme and the ancient city (*Figs. 18–22*). "The city is once more based on axes, as is every true architectural creation. Town planning enters into architecture and architecture into town planning. If the 'Voisin' plan is studied, there can be seen to the west and southwest the great openings made by Louis XIV, Louis XV, and Napoleon: the Invalides, the Tuileries, the Place de la Concorde, the Champ de Mars and the Étoile. These works are a signal example of *creation*, of that spirit which is able to dominate and compel the mob. Set in juxtaposition the new business city does not seem an anamoly, but rather gives the impression of being in the same tradition and following the normal laws of progress."[49]

As with all his planning schemes, Le Corbusier was at pains to indicate that his proposals were not visionary, but practical and financially sound, able not only to pay for themselves but to produce greatly augmented land values. If sufficient capital for the initial construction were not available in France, then foreign investment should be welcomed. "Are we to offer the center of Paris, with its noble sites and buildings, our national riches and splendour to Americans, English, Japanese or Germans? Yes, certainly."[50]

Although he seldom publicly wavered in support of even his most radical proposals, Le Corbusier realized that the total rebuilding of the historic center of Paris was unlikely to achieve favorable acceptance, and observed, "The 'Voisin' scheme does not claim to have found a final solution to the problem of the centre of Paris; but it may serve to raise the discussion to a level in keeping with the spirit of our age"[51] (*Fig. 25*).

GAP FORM 50A

SALESMAN'S ORDER

SALESMAN		DATE	6/3/77
SOLD TO		YOUR ORDER NO.	
STREET		TERMS	
CITY		SHIP VIA	

✓	QUAN.	PART NUMBER	DESCRIPTION	AMOUNT
	8	Zinc		7.75
	3	Clamps		1.20
	1	Bracket		1.00
	1	Reducer		1.00
	1	Fabric		6.00
				16.95

THE RADIANT CITY

In 1930, Le Corbusier received from officials in Moscow, where he had been at work on the Palace of Light Industry building (The Centrosoyus), a questionnaire regarding the reorganization of the Soviet capital. In formulating his answer, he submitted a series of drawings which constituted an elaboration of the principles of the City for Three Million, and which he termed the "Radiant City" (*Figs. 26–27*). Although the project had no discernible influence in the Soviet Union, it was exhibited at the Brussels meeting of the International Congresses of Modern Architecture (C.I.A.M.), and through wide publication served further to disseminate the ideas of its creator.

Although the new design maintained a rectilinear form, it differed from the City for Three Million in that it was developed along a central spine in such a way that the city could expand on either side. Le Corbusier admitted that a major defect of the previous design lay in its failure to provide for growth. The business district of widely spaced towers was retained, but moved to the upper edge of the city, below which would be the railroad terminal, carrying a rooftop airport. Below this, residential superblocks would flank a central civic axis, housing being restricted to apartment buildings of the setback type. An industrial zone containing parallel bands of factories, warehouses, and heavy industry would extend across the lower edge of the city, separated by a strip of parkland from the housing areas. This scheme eliminated the hierarchic population distribution and the Garden City suburbs of the City for Three Million.

The Radiant City scheme continued Le Corbusier's preoccupation with a biologically wholesome ambient. Urging both internal air-conditioning and external openness, he proclaimed the "reconstitution of a natural environment: *living air*, greenery and sky and the desired dose of sun on the skin; and, *in the lungs*, the living air of wide-open spaces."[52] The craving for sunlight inspired the ideal of a city in which no dwelling would face north, and prompted Le Corbusier eventually to change the design of the cruciform skyscraper to a concave slab in which the dominant facade would be oriented toward the south. Le Corbusier continually infused his writing with a vocabulary of organic imagery, basing the Radiant City on what he termed "the biological unit: the cell of 14 square meters per occupant."[53]

In later years he was to observe, "A *plan* arranges *organs* in order, thus creating *organism* or *organisms*. The organs possess distinctive qualities, specific differences. What are they? lungs, heart, stomach.... I am claiming sun, space and green surroundings for everybody and striving to provide you with an efficient system of circulation. BIOLOGY! The great new word in architecture and planning"[54] (*Fig. 32*).

In the Radiant City scheme, the principles established in the City for Three Million were developed in greater detail. The road system was designed on a 400 x 400 meter grid providing two-level elevated streets carrying heavy traffic at ground level and rapid motor traffic 5 meters above ground. Passages under the roads would be included for pedestrians and a system of tramways provided at ground level running parallel to the streets (*Figs. 29–31*).

The neighborhood-unit concept, which had been evolving during the 1920's, was reflected in a somewhat rudimentary way in the Radiant City scheme.[55] The population unit employed was 2,700 people—the number of residents employing a single entrance in an apartment block—and for this group would be provided, in addition to the communal domestic services, a nursery, kindergarten, and primary school. Although no commercial premises were included, the abundant sport facilities seen in the City for Three Million remained. Population density, based on the assumption of 14 square meters of dwelling space per inhabitant, was projected at 400 persons per acre (1,000 per hectare) (*Fig. 28*).

In advocating the virtues of an open urban fabric, Le Corbusier augmented his existing arguments with the contention that such a building pattern would be relatively resistant to aerial attack in time of war. His assumptions, of course, were based on the experience of World War I and the anticipation of aerial bombardment as it was conceived in the early 1930's.

The conventional city with its closely packed structures and narrow streets would suffer extensive damage through explosion and fire, while the corridor streets and courtyards would retain concentrations of poison gas. Within the Radiant City, however, the dispersed building pattern would make intensive damage less likely, while the water of the ubiquitous swimming pools would aid in firefighting. As the buildings would be raised above the ground on pilotis, poison gas would be dispersed by air currents. Residents of the buildings would take refuge not in underground shelters, but in the upper stories where the dangers of a direct hit would be mitigated through "metal plating providing definitive anti-bomb protection."[56]

As an architect, Le Corbusier's concern was first and foremost with the physical structure of the city, not with its complex social fabric, and one may easily complain that within the brave new world of mechanization and sun-cult athleticism idealized in his scheme there seems little place for the lame, the halt, the old or the poor. Just as Le Corbusier presupposed an "ideal" flat site in developing his generalized design, so he seems to have envisioned an "ideal" urban society, energetic, healthy, efficient, family, sport and work centered.

Le Corbusier was not altogether unaware, however, of a social imbalance in modern cities, believing that it was in part due to the presence of people lured from rural areas by the promise of better conditions, but who were perpetually unable to adjust or contribute constructively to urban life. Observing these misfits, he was "forced to the conclusion that our cities are bulging with human detritus, with the hordes of people who came to them to try their luck, did not succeed, and are now all huddled together in crowded slums. I knew we should have to say to them one day: there is nothing more for you to do in the city; there is no place for you here; go back where you came from, back to the country. And in that way the cities could be cleaned up."[57]

"The city must be cleared of all the dreams that have burned their wings, the miscarried lives, the dead embers of men and homes and communities that have accumulated around the city's bright furnace and are now stifling it with their dead and sooty weight. [58]

The solution to the problem, Le Corbusier concluded, lay in a revitalization of the countryside to provide the rural citizenry with the advantages of modern living. He appears to have been motivated through association with an agricultural laborer, Norbert Bézard, who had written to him complaining, "There is a fog of disease and despair eating away our very hearts, out here in the country. The French countryside is sick and dying. Corbusier, you must build us the 'Radiant Farm,' the 'Radiant Village.'"[59]

In spite of his fondness for modernization, Le Corbusier did not regard large-scale mechanized farming as suitable for France. The Radiant Farm design which he produced maintained the traditional family farm unit provided with a standardized house on pilotis, a modern barn, and animal and machinery sheds (*Fig. 33*). Describing the scheme, Le Corbusier maintained, "The entire conception of this farmhouse is dominated by esthetic and ethical factors: light, cleanliness, immaculate domestic equipment. Once he has been provided with a tool so modern and so cleanly designed, the peasant will come to love it and look after it as well as he does his horse or his pig."[60]

Contemplating the countryside as a whole, Le Corbusier foresaw a new era of communication based on the highway, predicting that "the automobile would bring life back to the places that the railroad had cut off, and that a new relationship, a living and supple one, could be established between the city and the country, between the city dweller and the country dweller: a unity of spirit."[61] In redesigning the country village, Le Corbusier considered the town as "fundamentally and inescapably a function of the transportation system, of storage needs, of merchandise handling problems."[62] The Radiant Village (*Fig. 34*) presupposed a system of rural cooperatives and would include a communal silo, machinery storehouse and a cooperative store. A village club would provide a center for communal life, and an apartment house would replace the single-family housing of the traditional village. With characteristic optimism, Le Corbusier concluded, "When we have done all this, then the land will attract people back to it naturally. *We shall not be able to empty the cities of their superfluous population until the land has been materially and spiritually redeveloped*. When it has, then it will attract all the people who are unsuited to city life back again."[63]

VARIATIONS ON A THEME

The first major summation of Le Corbusier's ideas on city planning was contained in his book *Urbanisme* (*City of To-morrow*), published in 1925. Having thus presented his design concepts and theories, he assured his readers, "I do not propose to bear witness in the highways and byways as though I belonged to the Salvation Army."[64] This, however, is precisely what he did with unflagging conviction and for the length of his career, tirelessly entering every available competition, repeatedly offering his services to government officials, producing a prolix stream of theoretical writing, and promulgating his ideas through worldwide lecturing.

Through the years Le Corbusier achieved increasing renown as an architect, and although unrealized, through constant reiteration, his urban designs achieved a cliché-like familiarity. He was continually active in the International Congresses of Modern Architecture (C.I.A.M.), employing the meetings of this organization as a platform for his views, and seeing many of his principles embodied in the Charter of Athens of 1933. This document, which exemplified the growing consciousness among architects of the importance of city planning, attempted to codify standards for urban design, considering the city in terms of four functions: dwelling, work, cultivation of mind and body, and circulation. As Le Corbusier reminded his colleagues, "Town planning is the crucial centre of all our problems."[65]

Le Corbusier led A.S.C.O.R.A.L., the French section of C.I.A.M. (Assemblée de Constructeurs pour une Rénovation Architecturale), and this group, under his direction, was responsible for incorporating the principles of the Athens Charter into the C.I.A.M. grid, a device for the visual presentation of material relating to city planning (*Fig. 35*). The grid consisted of a series of display panels on which illustrative material could be mounted, organized according to prescribed categories. Information was coordinated on the grid in terms of four horizontal divisions: dwelling, work, cultivation of mind and body, and circulation. These parallel presentations were grouped under headings relating to the environment, site planning, built volume, equipment, ethics and aesthetics, social and economic factors, legislation, and steps in realization. The grid was employed to display more than twenty town plans at the C.I.A.M. meeting at Bergamo, Italy, in 1949.

Throughout the 1930's Le Corbusier continued to apply his theories to a wide variety of unbuilt projects, among which were a competition design for the urbanization of the Norrmalm and Sodermalm districts of Stockholm (1933), a master plan for Barcelona (1932), and a design for a Bata shoe manufacturing center in Lorraine at Hellocourt (1935).

Employing the principles of the Radiant City, Le Corbusier entered a competition scheme, in 1933, for the left bank of the Scheldt in Antwerp, reporting that the submitted 40 meters of drawings had received only the briefest consideration before the jury pronounced the verdict, "lunatics" (*Figs. 36–37*). Also unsuccessful was a city plan proposed for Nemours in Algeria (1934), a city projected as the sea terminus of a new railway from Fez in Morocco, and being developed as a port (*Figs. 38–39*). Assuming visual dominance in this scheme was a residential district of high-rise apartment slabs on an elevated site overlooking the sea, which Le Corbusier likened to an amphitheater. He pointed out that the overall master plan, which involved zoning the city into an industrial district, a civic and tourist center, and a business city was "on all points in conformity with the Athens Charter of CIAM."[66]

Although the Voisin Plan for Paris had aroused no particular enthusiasm when exhibited in 1925, Le Corbusier continued to elaborate schemes for his native city, convinced that the salvation of the French capital lay in a redevelopment of its center according to his principles. Deploring the existing state of the city, he maintained, "I can say now that Paris fills me with despair. That once admirable city has nothing left inside it but the soul of an archeologist. No more power of command. No head. No powers of action. No genius."[67] Parisian officialdom remained unmoved; however, Le Corbusier observed toward the end of his life, "Since 1922 (for the past 42 years) I have continued to work, in general and in detail, on the problem of Paris. Everything has been made public. The City Council has never contacted me. It calls me 'Barbarian'!"[68]

Meanwhile, whatever hopes Le Corbusier may have had of influencing the Soviets to adopt his civic designs were obliterated through a combination of factors, including a government policy of urban decentralization which had prevailed during the 1920's, coupled with an official condemnation of modern design promulgated in the early 1930's. In the period immediately following the revolution, the large central city had been viewed as a bourgeois survival, and Le Corbusier's visionary schemes could be seen as symbolic manifestations of capitalist exploitation. Le Corbusier had insisted, "I am an architect; no one is going to make a politician of me,"[69] replying to Communist criticism of the City for Three Million by stressing that he had sought only to solve a technical problem, but that he had been "severely criticized because I had not labelled the finest buildings on my plan 'People's Hall,' 'Soviet,' or 'Syndicalist Hall,' and so on; and because I did not crown my plan with the slogan 'Nationalization of all property.'"[70]

Le Corbusier had submitted his Radiant City scheme to the Soviets with the declaration that "The cornerstone of modern urbanization is absolute respect for the freedom of the individual," without realizing that "Such words, such a thought, such an act, are anathema in Moscow."[71] Not only did such statements run counter to collectivist doctrine, but the technical innovation of universal air conditioning urged by the architect was deemed a morbid escapist fantasy antithetical to the wholesome realities of Soviet society, and prompted the verdict that Le Corbusier had "consulted none other than [H. G.] Wells about the problems of urban organization."[72]

However revolutionary Le Corbusier may have seemed in some circles, to the Soviet Commissar for Culture, Lunacharsky, he was "a bourgeois intellectual sitting in an airconditioned office, looking at the world through horn-rimmed spectacles";[73] and although the Radiant City scheme had been initiated as a proposal for Moscow, a copy of *La ville radieuse* sent by the publisher to Voks in 1935, was returned as having "no interest for the U.S.S.R."[74]

Le Corbusier's predilection for apartment housing and elevated motor freeways produced a poetic variant in his urban designs during a trip to South America in 1929. Invited to give a series of lectures in Buenos Aires, he projected a scheme of urban development for this city in which a new high-rise business center and airport would be constructed on extensions into the Rio de la Plata (*Fig. 44*). He then continued his travels, producing sketch plans for Montevideo (*Fig. 40*) and São Paulo (*Fig. 41*), and culminated his trip with a public appearance in Rio de Janeiro.[75]

Although Le Corbusier's generalized urban schemes had presupposed flat sites to facilitate the application of geometric plans free of topographic constraints, when confronted with the irregular configurations of actual sites, he was often moved to his most imaginative and effective efforts. Defining the urban designer, he once wrote, "The modeller of towns, the organizer gathers, assimilates, comprises within himself the whole countryside and the whole topography."[76] One of Le Corbusier's greatest talents included a matchless sense of natural scale; he once described his approach to design as beginning. "with the acoustic of the landscape, taking as a starting point the four horizons."[77]

In Rio de Janeiro the dramatic meeting of mountains and sea stimulated Le Corbusier to a design approach no longer conceived as "an operation directed against nature," but as a balanced and harmonious interplay of powerful man-made and natural forms. Like most visitors, he was rhapsodic about the beauty of Rio. "The sea, the bay opening toward the sea filled with islands and promontories; the mountains which lift themselves toward the sky tempestuously, carving out innumerable shifting vistas—a sort of tumultuous green flame above the city, always, everywhere, changing aspect with each step.... Here in Rio de Janeiro, a city which seems radiantly to defy all human collaboration in its universally proclaimed beauty, I have the strong desire, a bit mad, perhaps, to attempt here a human adventure—the desire to set up a duality, to create 'the affirmation of man' against or with 'the presence of nature.'"[78]

26

This affirmation would take the form of an immense motor freeway 100 meters high, stretching through the city linking major points and containing apartments within the structure below the roadway (*Figs. 42–43*). Le Corbusier claimed that the whole freeway could be built without in any way interfering with the city below, as only the concrete supports would require ground space, and the apartments would begin 30 meters above the ground, presumably clearing all existing rooftops. Between this 30-meter level and the 100-meter height of the roadway ten double stories of apartments could be provided, with descent for vehicles to the streets below to be made by elevator.

The romantic aspects of the scheme prompted Le Corbusier to lyricize that he had created in his elevated apartments "almost the nest of a bird planner.... The airplane will become jealous of such liberties which seemed to be reserved for him."[79] He proclaimed that the tumultuous peaks of Rio would be exalted by contrast with the great continuous band of building. "The steamers which pass, magnificent and moving structures of modern times, will find there, suspended in the space above the city, a response, an echo, an answer. The entire site begins to speak, of the water, of the land, of the air: it speaks architecture. This discourse is a poem of human geometry and an immense fantasy of nature. The eye sees two things: nature and the product of human labor. The city announces itself by a line which, alone, is capable of harmonizing with the violent caprice of the mountains: the horizontal.[80]

The concept of the elevated highway incorporating housing which had been initially sketched for Rio was adapted in a more comprehensive manner for Algiers between 1930 and 1933[81] (*Figs. 45–49*). As planned Projects A and B would have involved the creation of a motor freeway 100 meters high following the mountainous coastline to link the suburbs of Hussein-Dey and Saint-Eugène with the central city, the substructure of the roadway to be developed as housing for approximately 180,000 people (*Figs. 46–49*). Abandoning his previous insistence on unity of detail and standardized dwellings, Le Corbusier conceived of the floor levels of the structure as "artificial sites" (*Fig. 47*), units for construction which would be purchased and designed according to the owner's wishes. Within the megastructure of the elevated road, "Every architect will build his villa as he likes; what does it matter to the whole if a Moorish-style villa flanks another in Louis XVIth or in Italian Renaissance?"[82]

In addition to the coastline freeway, Le Corbusier also proposed development of an elevated site adjacent to the city, the Fort-l'Empereur district, which would contain a complex of curving apartment blocks housing 200,000 people, and connected directly to a new high-rise business center by means of an elevated roadway (*Fig. 49*). Convinced as always of the desirability of his plan from both an aesthetic and practical point of view, Le Corbusier made repeated efforts to convince government officials of its economic soundness, eventually reducing his proposals to the detailed development of a new waterfront business center (Project C, 1934). Unable to achieve favorable consideration of even this relatively modest scheme, he left Algiers ruminating gloomily on shipboard, "Now the 'De Grasse' is on the open sea. Algiers drops out of sight, like a magnificent body, supple-hipped and full-breasted, but covered by the sickening scabs of a skin disease. A body which could be revealed in all its magnificence, through the judicious influence of form and the bold use of mathematics to harmonize natural topography and human geometry. But I have been expelled, the doors have been shut in my face. I am leaving and deeply I feel: I am right, I am right, I am right."[83]

The following year, 1935, Le Corbusier made his first visit to the United States, a country which he had long regarded with mixed feelings. Although he respected American pioneering in the development of high-rise building, he had employed illustrations of American cities in his books as examples of brutally chaotic, unplanned urban growth (*Figs. 51–52*). To a large extent his observations in the United States confirmed views already held.

Le Corbusier admired the vigor, optimism and energy which he felt animated American life; he praised American cleanliness, technical sophistication and efficiency; he was sensitive to the unique beauties of American cities; yet he found himself frequently appalled by what seemed the life-denying qualities of the overall urban environment. "A hundred times I have thought: New York is a catastrophe, and fifty times: it is a beautiful catastrophe."[84]

Although Le Corbusier gave many lectures during his American visit, his most famous comment occurred during an interview upon arrival, when his answer to the inevitable question, "What do you think of New York?" produced in the *New York Herald Tribune* the headlines

FINDS AMERICAN SKYSCRAPERS MUCH TOO SMALL
Skyscrapers not big enough
Says Le Corbusier at first sight
Thinks they should be huge and a lot farther apart.[85]

Erected as part of no overall plan and crowded on congested sites, New York skyscrapers seemed to Le Corbusier "sublime, naïve, touching, idiotic."[86]

"The skyscrapers were not constructed with a wise and serious intention. They were applauded acrobatic feats. The *skyscraper as a proclamation* won. Here the skyscraper is not an element in city planning, but a banner in the sky, a fireworks rocket, an aigrette in the coiffure of a name henceforth listed in the financial Almanach de Gotha."[87]

Although he admired the efficiency of American mass transport, Le

Corbusier deplored the economic and human waste involved in large-scale commuting. "They constructed Pullmans, subways, highways, roads, and covered the country with swarms of automobiles. The country is on wheels; everything rolls. You are free because you are on the road at the wheel of your own car, because you can read the paper on the train! Industry is kept busy in creating this gigantic mass of machinery. I think that it is an illness. I said: 'Yes, the cancer is in good health.'"[88] In addition to deploring the time, expense, and fatigue involved in lengthy daily travel, he saw the suburban pattern as one which fragmented the family, necessitating long hours of separation and possible estrangement between husband and wife.

Le Corbusier was in many ways prophetic regarding problems which would ultimately become acute in American cities. He foresaw the dangers of emptying the central city of its middle-class population, describing the circumstances which made such people increasingly oblivious to central urban problems. He observed, "I scarcely more than glimpsed the slums of New York and I believe that New Yorkers never see them on their daily rounds; they are unaware of them. If they knew the slums, it would make them sick at heart and they would make new city plans. For the world needs city planning in order to conquer human misery."[89]

Although Le Corbusier was often accused of a lack of concern for the human aspect of cities, his comments sometimes revealed an acute social observation. "Americans are eminently democratic—except about Negroes and that is a very grave question which cannot be resolved in a superficial way.... The misery of our times comes from the fact that those who rule are those who have succeeded and who, consequently and quite naturally, live in conditions of material well-being. Inevitably, in spite of themselves and despite an evident good will, they are ignorant of the great charnel house of human misery."[90]

Summing up his impressions, Le Corbusier termed the United States the "country of timid people," a land where in spite of enormous wealth and technical competence, the capacity for truly bold action in the solution of urban problems seemed lacking.

Although the Second World War brought with it a cessation of architectural commissions, Le Corbusier, in semiretirement, continued to develop urban schemes and publish theoretical writing. He elaborated his plan for Buenos Aires (1938), and developed a final scheme for Algiers (1942)—a pilot plan outlining an evolutionary development for the city until 1980 (*Figs. 50, 53–54*). In this scheme, he envisioned Algiers in terms of two physical and cultural spheres, the Moslem and the European (*Figs. 55–56*). The Marine district (*Fig. 57*) adjacent to the Casbah would be given over to Moslem cultural institutions, and where this area joined the European city, a new civic center would be built.

A new circulation system for the city was projected, giving access to the heights which would be developed with high-rise apartments, although the earlier conception of an elevated freeway incorporating apartments below the roadway was abandoned.

In his theoretical work, although his general conceptions of urban form remained relatively consistent, Le Corbusier began to direct his attention to a larger environmental scale, envisioning patterns of regional development, and considering the "frame of a mechanized civilization" in terms of three "human establishments": the agricultural unit, the linear-industrial city, and the radio-concentric city (*Fig. 58*). The latter represented the traditional centralized city functioning as a center of distribution, administration, and culture. Stretching between such urban centers would be lines of transportation along which would be developed a linear pattern of industrial-residential complexes (*Fig. 60–61*). As schematically conceived, each "green factory" employing about 3,500 workers would be sited in open space along lines of rail, road, and water transportation, and separated from the residential district by a landscaped highway (*Fig. 62*). Within the residential area would be both high- and low-rise housing, together with community facilities.

Although Le Corbusier had previously chosen the redevelopment of the central city as the primary focus of his efforts, he had evidently become convinced that revitalization of urban centers could be accomplished only within a larger conception of planned settlement. Le Corbusier's linear proposals had no specific economic base, but were projected on an arbitrary framework of transportation, the "four routes" of water, railroad, highway, and air. He considered a linear pattern of dispersal superior to other systems of decentralization, maintaining, "We must save ourselves from the easy hypnosis of satellite towns. Here, henceforth, along the great arteries for the passage of merchandise would be sited the lawful satellite towns—the new centres of industry. Along the canals, which they will punctuate, the linear cities of industry will be established. Factories will be shifted towards their designated sites. The conditions of nature will have been realized in the workshops and in the dwellings."[91]

In a vision reminiscent of Soria y Mata (1844–1920), Le Corbusier visualized the whole of Europe with a configuration of linear settlement, conceiving a major linear city extending east-west from the Atlantic to the Urals and intersected by north-south axes of similar settlement[92] (*Fig. 59*). The linear scheme was intended to counteract what Le Corbusier regarded as an outmoded and ruinous pattern of urban development engendered by the railroad in the nineteenth century. He observed that, "In a hundred years a technical civilization is born, disruptive in its power and its possibilities, upsetting everything in its passage.... A revolution in circumstances, in lives, in institutions. A black wretchedness, a black disorder: men suddenly lose their water-level and their plumb line.... The tentacular cities were born; Paris, London, New York, Rio de Janeiro, Buenos Aires. The countryside was emptied. Here was a double catastrophe. A menacing loss of equilibrium."[93]

The linear city conception as a means of decentralization and industrial dispersal had been earlier considered in the Soviet Union; Le Corbusier's design bore a schematic resemblance to N. A. Miliutin's Stalingrad plan of 1930, in which the industrial district paralleled a railroad line, and was separated from the residential district by a band of greenery containing a motor highway. The Soviet scheme had represented an attempt to minimize the differences between the urban and rural proletariat by having both classes relate to the same linear city. Le Corbusier, however, felt this population mixture unsuitable to the nature of agricultural and industrial work, observing that "the farm worker is bound by an annual rhythm (365 days, and the four seasons, year after year); the industrial worker by the solar law of a twenty-four hour day."[94]

The agricultural establishment as projected by Le Corbusier would consist of individual farming units and cooperative villages continuing the conceptions of the Radiant Farm and Radiant Village schemes of the 1930's. The rural establishment would be dependent on road transportation, but would also contain autogyro bases within the villages for rapid communication to major airports (*Fig. 63*).

Le Corbusier envisioned the new urban pattern as a way to free the central city from excessive pressures of growth, and from the undesirable encumbrance of manufacturing activity. "The parasitic fringes of the cultural centres are cut away and re-grafted as linear cities; the centres of culture shine again, returned to their natural order."[95] Cities, he felt, should control their growth through a selectivity of function, "recognizing their true reason for being, eliminating that which has no reason to be attached to them," and he reiterated the view that urban centres should be purged of undesirable people. "They must repudiate their parasitic populations, which have thrust themselves in to participate in an adventure crowned with failure. They must decrease."[96]

With the end of the war, and the resulting period of reconstruction, Le Corbusier resumed production of unbuilt urban designs. For the bombed town of Saint Dié (1946), he produced a scheme involving the creation of a new civic center flanked by a series of large apartment houses in the central part of the town, with a rebuilt industrial district on the opposite side of a river (*Figs. 64–65*). Although the design was exhibited and praised in the United States and Canada, it found no acceptance in France, sharing the fate of plans for the redevelopment of La Rochelle-Pallice (1945–1946), Saint-Gaudens (1945–1946), and Meaux (1956–1957) (*Fig. 72*).

For Marseilles Le Corbusier had produced a redevelopment plan together with a "vertical garden city" scheme for South Marseilles, a projected ensemble of apartment houses sited within open space

(*Figs. 66–69*). Of this project, he succeeded in constructing only a single apartment block, which he termed "l'Unité d'Habitation," a building designed to provide its 1,600 inhabitants with a number of communal facilities, functioning in itself as a small neighborhood unit (*Fig. 70*).

In his conception of communal living, Le Corbusier claimed to have been influenced by monastic society. "The key... appearing again after fifty years, was the visit to the Carthusian Monastery at Ema in Tuscany in 1907: the appearance of a possible harmony, fashioned a thousand years before, but transposable to the present since involving the indissoluble binomial—'individual collectivity.' The monastery of Ema has shown the way."[97] It is also possible to see a relation between the Unité conception and the phalanstery community projected by Charles Fourier (1772–1837) in the nineteenth century. A visionary theorist, Fourier had imagined his ideal community as consisting of a "phalanx" (*phalanstère*) of 1,620 people housed within a single building and sharing many aspects of collective living.[98]

Within the Unité d'Habitation, as initially projected by Le Corbusier, half the seventh and eighth floors were allocated to a large cooperative store, individual shops and laundry facilities. A small restaurant was also to be provided, together with an eighteen-room hotel designed to accommodate guests of the tenants. The seventeenth floor was to contain a nursery and kindergarten, while the roof would have a wading pool and playspace for small children. Also on the roof was an open-air gymnasium, a 300-meter running track, and a solarium. Not all the projected facilities were successfully realized, however, and the placement of extensive commercial premises within the building proved to be economically unsound. Observing the abandoned interior shopping street, one critic commented, "Its failure was inevitable; Le Corbusier overlooked the fact that a population three times the size of Unity House's was needed to support the shops and services he made room for."[99]

The apartment units were based on a standardized dwelling-type evolved from the "freehold maisonette" (*Immeubles-Villas*) apartments of Le Corbusier's early urban designs, and he liked to describe these units as fitting into the framework of the structure like bottles into a rack (*Fig. 71*). Although the Unité involved no technical innovations, his visual representations of the Marseilles apartments were somewhat prophetic of the current conception of "plug-in" architecture, in which small independent units can be fitted into a larger megastructure.

Le Corbusier was convinced that the Unité type of housing represented a universally applicable solution to the problem of urban dwelling, regarding the Marseilles block as a prototype which could subsequently be adapted to standardized mass production. He succeeded, however, in realizing only three other buildings of this type, one

1. The Acropolis, sketched by Le Corbusier."If the Acropolis of Athens has a destiny, it is to cradle between Mount Pentelicus and Mount Hymettus the very sound of the voice of man and the justification of the actions of man" (*The Radiant City*, 1935). "The Greeks on the Acropolis set up temples which are animated by a single thought, drawing around them the desolate landscape and gathering it into the composition. Thus, on every point of the horizon, the thought is single" (*Towards a New Architecture*, 1923).

"The Roman city is a city of ORDER. Disciplined, hierarchic, dignified. And the Roman camp too already possessed the same qualities. It was disciplined, hierarchic, dignified… The Romans built WHOLES. The creations of their architects and city planners were invariably WHOLES… They conceived, they classified, they reduced everything to order: Rome meant enterprise… They were lucid, strong, simple and geometrical. They created cities that worked like machines: machines of which the product was action" (*The Radiant City*).

2. Roman ruins sketched by Le Corbusier.

3. The town of Rouen based on a Roman plan, sketched by Le Corbusier.

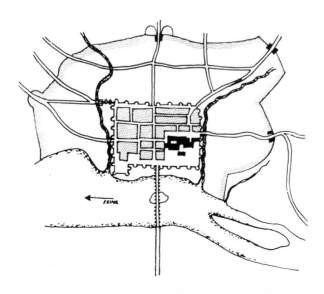

4. Piazza San Marco, sketched by Le Corbusier. "Here—Venice, Saint Mark's Square set with the bright diamonds of successive epochs.... All these techniques, these different materials. But each newcomer had a faith in his own adventure and, taking stock of his neighbors, risked... dared.... Kings have made of classicism a symbol of gentility, of loftiness of mind, and sometimes of the iron glove. Of gentility above all: an air of indifference and dispassionate calm; of civility, in which all is proportioned to the human scale, without emphasis. This great manifestation of measure resulted from the exercise of a supreme force, of will; today the feeble brandish its souvenirs about them ... substitutes for the present exercise of force, of will, of measuring up to the scale of our times.... Take life from classicism, nothing remains but a formula: academicism" (*Concerning Town Planning*, 1946).

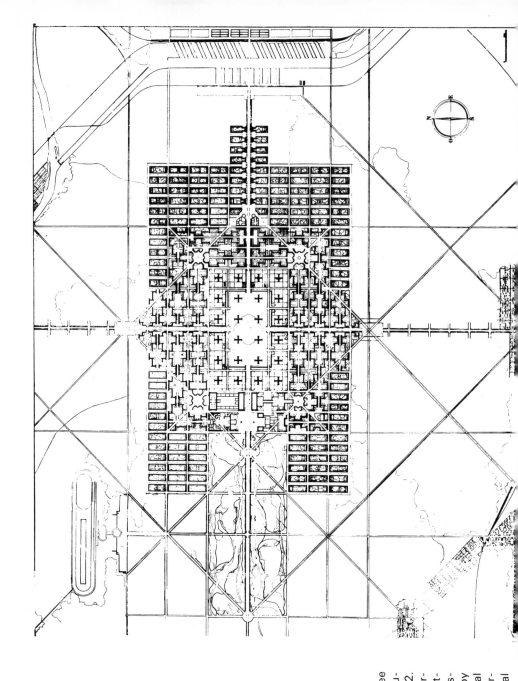

5. Plan of a Contemporary City for Three
Million People, exhibited by Le Corbusier at the Salon d'Automne in 1922.
The rectilinear central city is surrounded by a wide greenbelt and outlying "Garden Cities." Industrial district is at right. The center is marked by
a transportation hub and commercial
district of cruciform skyscrapers, surrounding which are the residential

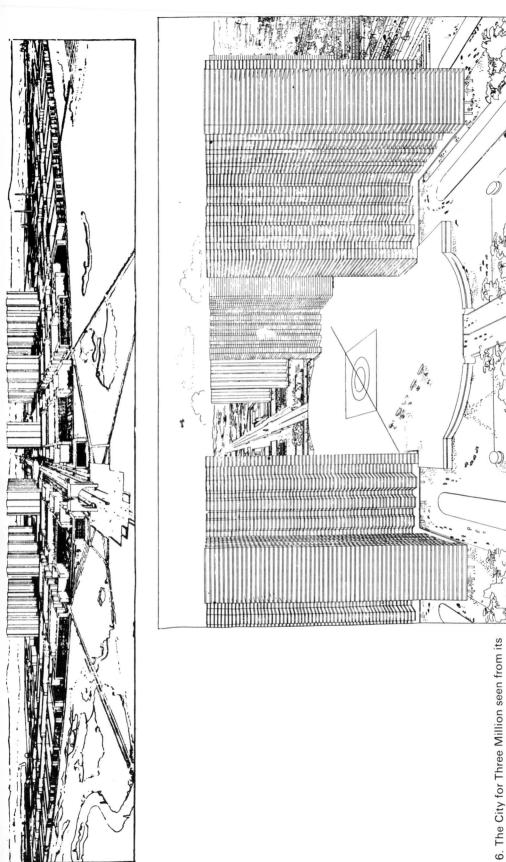

6. The City for Three Million seen from its surrounding greenbelt.

7. View of the central station and airport of the City for Three Million with adjacent skyscraper office buildings.

8. "The 'City' seen from the main road, left and right the administration buildings, in the background the museums and universities."

9. "The center of the City seen from the terrace of one of the café tiers which surround the station plaza. One views the station between the two skyscrapers at left, elevated slightly above ground. Leaving the station one sees the motor freeway extending to the right toward the English Garden. We are in the center of the city, where the density and circulation are at the highest. The terraces of the tiered cafés constitute the frequented boulevards. The theaters, public halls, and so on, are within the spaces between the skyscrapers, in the midst of trees"—author's translation (*Oeuvre complète 1910–29*).

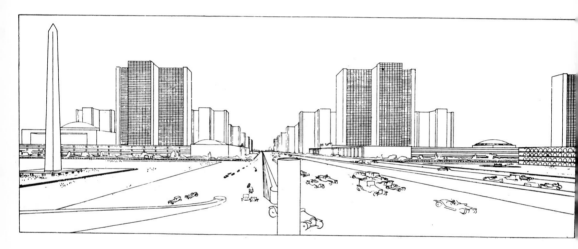

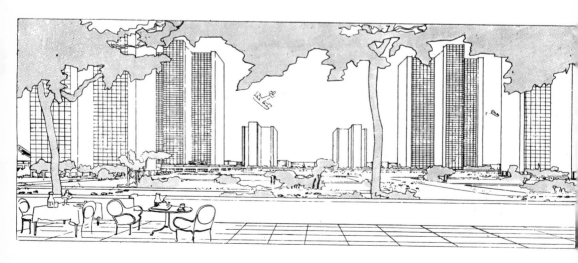

10. View of the residential superblocks showing apartment houses that extend across the streets of the inner residential zone of the city. Le Corbusier frequently referred to high-rise dwellings set amid open space as "vertical garden cities."

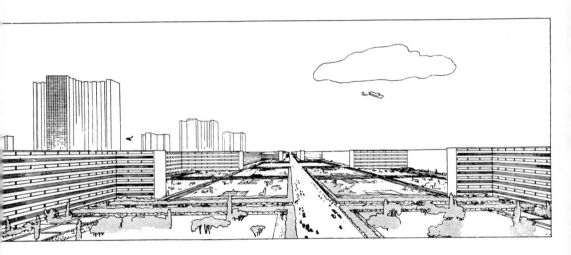

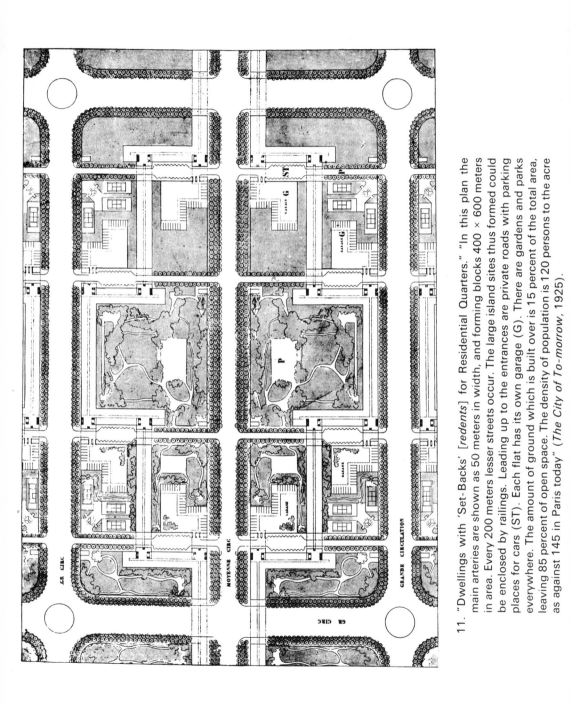

11. "Dwellings with 'Set-Backs' [*redents*] for Residential Quarters." "In this plan the main arteries are shown as 50 meters in width, and forming blocks 400 × 600 meters in area. Every 200 meters lesser streets occur. The large island sites thus formed could be enclosed by railings. Leading up to the entrances are private roads with parking places for cars (ST). Each flat has its own garage (G). There are gardens and parks everywhere. The amount of ground which is built over is 15 percent of the total area, leaving 85 percent of open space. The density of population is 120 persons to the acre as against 145 in Paris today" (*The City of To-morrow*, 1925).

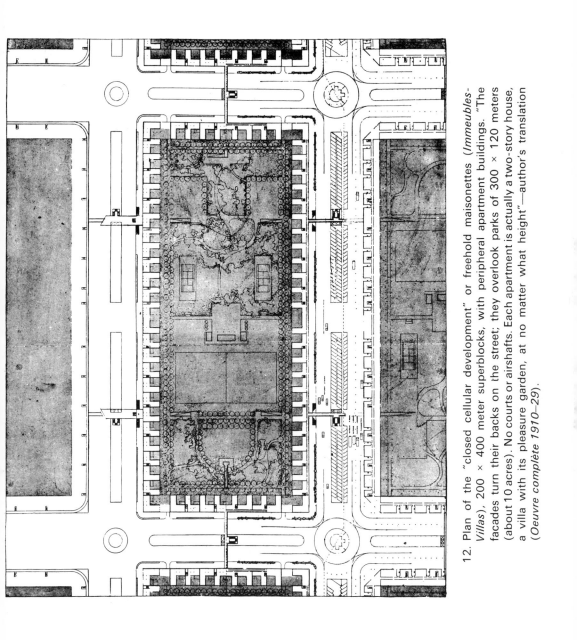

12. Plan of the "closed cellular development" or freehold maisonettes (*Immeubles-Villas*), 200 × 400 meter superblocks, with peripheral apartment buildings. "The facades turn their backs on the street; they overlook parks of 300 × 120 meters (about 10 acres). No courts or airshafts. Each apartment is actually a two-story house, a villa with its pleasure garden, at no matter what height"—author's translation (*Oeuvre complète 1910–29*).

13. Detail of apartment façade. Each dwelling unit contains a two-story living room with adjacent terrace.

14. Sketch by Le Corbusier of the freehold-maisonette concept applied to an unbuilt scheme for Geneva, 1928–1929.

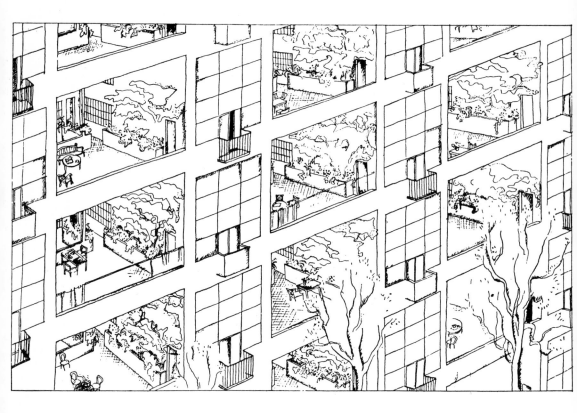

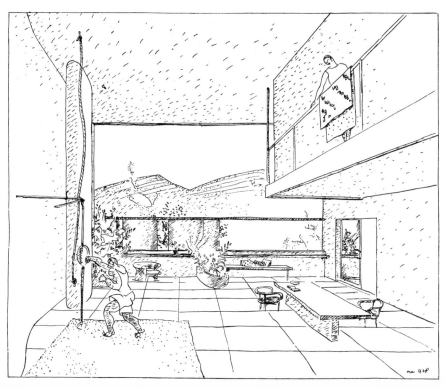

15. "We state the problem quite logically: dwelling 50 m², pleasure garden 50 m² (this garden and this dwelling are situated at ground level or at 6 or 12 meters above the ground) in "cellular" groupings. At the foot of the dwellings, the vast sport grounds (soccer, tennis, and so on) at the rate of 150 m² per dwelling"—author's translation (*Oeuvre complète 1910–29*). Garden allotments would also be provided.

Above: "Cellular" development proposed for the Garden Cities.
Bottom left: House type.
Bottom right: Plan.

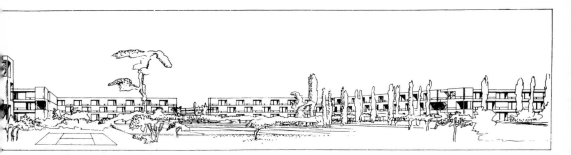

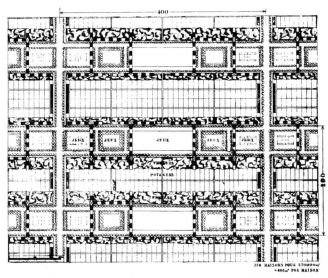

THE VOISIN PLAN

16. Le Corbusier saw Paris as a disorderly accretion within which had been developed a series of classically ordered complexes.

17. "Paris: The Cité, The Place Dauphine, L'Île Saint-Louis, The Invalides, L'École Militaire. A significant diagram. These outline drawings, which are all to the same scale, show the trend towards order. The town is being policed, culture is manifesting itself and Man is able to create" (*The City of To-morrow*).

18. 1925 sketch of the renovated center of Paris. The Île de la Cité appears at left.

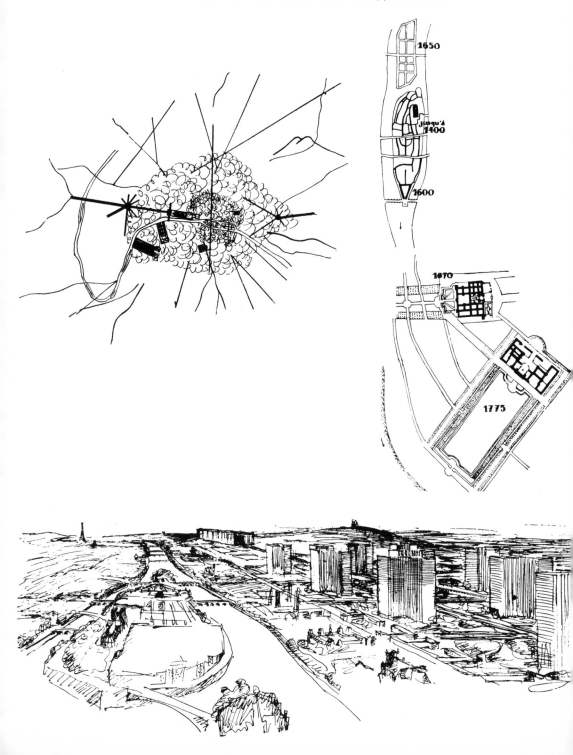

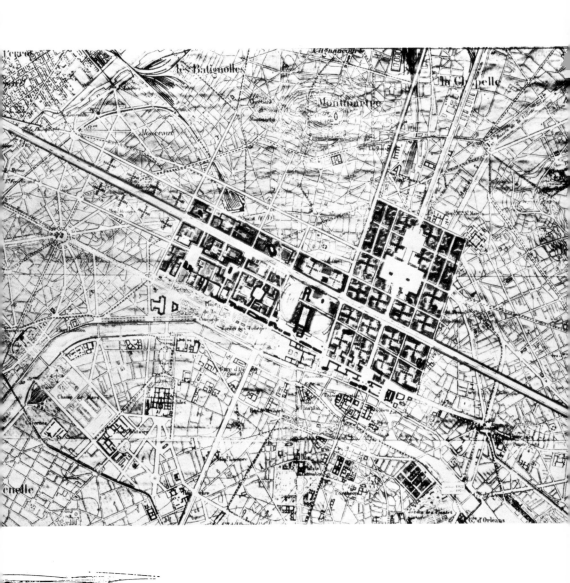

20. 1930 model for the center of Paris. The Louvre appears at bottom center, and the Île de la Cité at right. "The axis of the undertaking was well chosen: you can see the Tour Saint-Jacques, which has been spared.

"Above, in the future *place*, you see the Porte Saint-Denis and Porte Saint-Martin. "From right to left, from east to west, you see the 'great East-West throughway of Paris' which embodies the future of Paris and offers the City Council the chance to launch a gigantic financial enterprise, a 'money-making' enterprise = a source of wealth" (*The Radiant City*, 1935).

21. The urban scale of the Voisin Plan shown juxtaposed against that of the surrounding area.

22. Sketch by Le Corbusier attemping to demonstrate a similarity in scale and form between his own building conceptions and historic Parisian complexes. "History bequeaths us objects of admiration of which the scale and appearance are for us an inexhaustible source of joy....The Place Vendôme. The Court of the Louvre, The Place de la Concorde. The propositions of modern urbanism have led to a dimensioning of undertakings and an organization of site which re-establish the same scale. Happy recognition of the human scale in its most dignified aspects. It is for us to create beauty through a grandeur of spirit, through unity"—author's translation (*Oeuvre complète 1938–46*).

23. Sketch of Paris showing new motor arteries proposed by Le Corbusier. The east-west axis was intended to relieve the Champs Élysées of its traffic burden. "And should it happen, in Paris, for example, that the bed of certain vital routes has been allowed to become encrusted by the narrow walls of history, a surgical operation will trace a new bed parallel to the first, capable of handling modern speeds, with no damage to our inheritance from the past" (*The Home of Man*, 1941).

24. The Champs Élysées shown preserved as a triumphal route, with the new circulation axis established parallel to it.

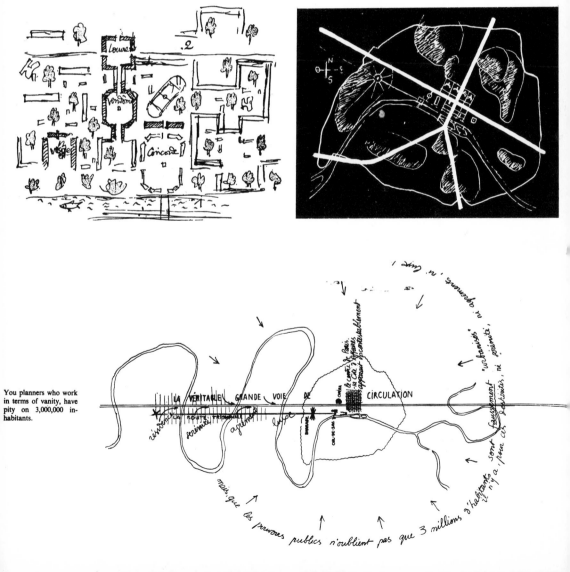

You planners who work in terms of vanity, have pity on 3,000,000 inhabitants.

25. "Paris was transformed on its own ground, without evasion. Each current of thought is inscribed in its stones, throughout the centuries. In this way the living image of Paris was formed. Paris must continue!" (*The Radiant City*).

6. The Radiant City designed in 1930. Business district is at top, with circular station complex directly beneath. Residential superblocks flank a central commercial and civic axis, while industrial complexes are sited below. The plan provides for lateral expansion on either side of the central axis. "Modern society is throwing off its rags and preparing to move into a new home: the Radiant city" (*The Radiant City*, 1935).

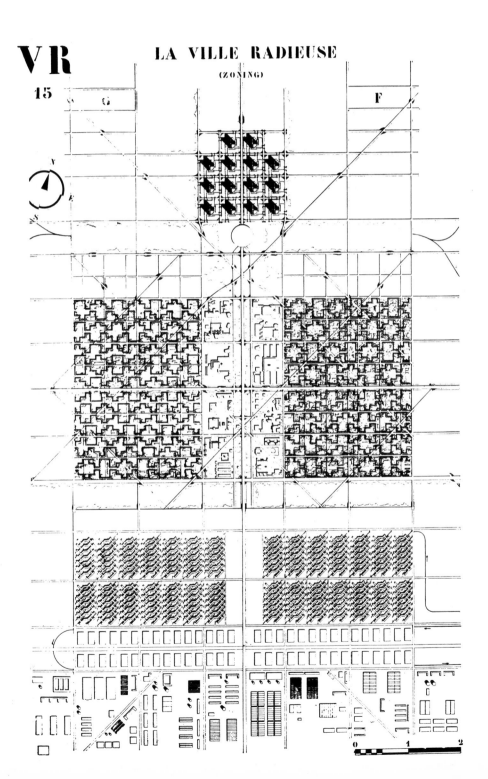

27. The building pattern of the Radiant City compared, at the same scale, with Paris (left), New York (center), and Buenos Aires (right).

28. Residential superblocks of the Radiant City. Rapid motor traffic would be restricted to the 400 × 400 meter grid surrounding the sectors. Apartment housing, designed in a series of setbacks [*redents*] that form an independent pattern transcending the elevated highway grid, would be sited amid parks and athletic facilities; population density would be 400 per acre based on a unit of 14 square meters of floorspace per inhabitant—more than three times as great as in his earlier project. The abundant landscaping prompted Le Corbusier to call his scheme the "Green City." 1. Swimming pool. 2. Soccer. 3. Tennis. 4. Playground.

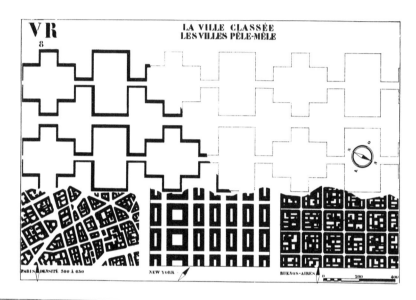

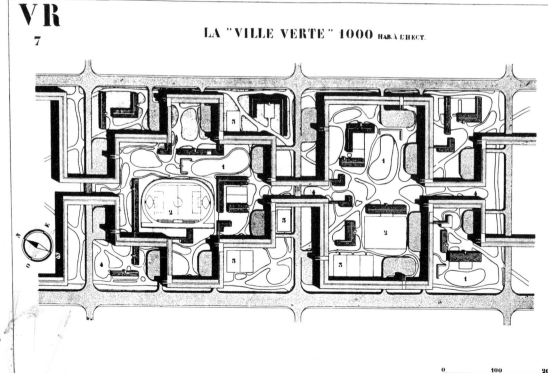

29. Road sections from the Radiant City, 1930. Automobile traffic would be carried on a roadway elevated 5 meters above ground. Heavy traffic would move at ground level, with underpasses provided for pedestrians.

30a and b. "Comparative sections of a Radiant City apartment house and a traditional Parisian apartment house. In the former: Sun, space, trees, man returned to fundamental conditions: contact with nature. In the latter: The 'corridor street'; the apartment on the street or courts, without expanse in front. Unmerciful in aerial warfare"—author's translation (*Oeuvre complète 1934–38*).

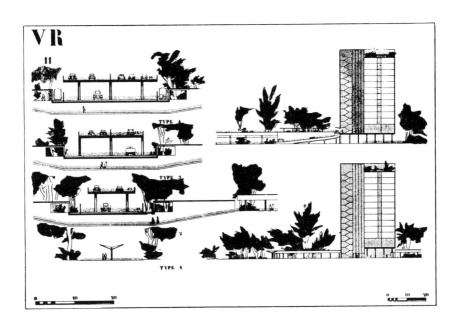

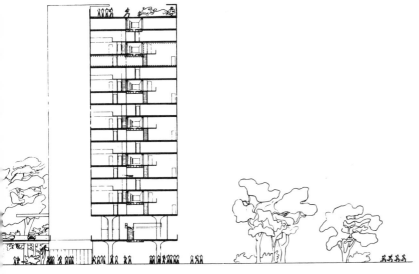

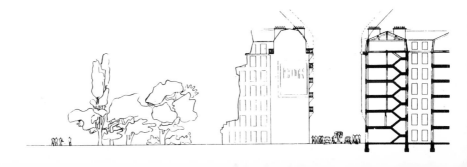

31. Model of the Radiant City showing apartment blocks and elevated roadways.

32. Le Corbusier's conception of the "Green City" sketched in Buenos Aires in 1929. "In the heart of the business city where the skyscrapers raise their heads, the town still remains green. The trees are kings; men, under their cover, live in the domain of proportion; the link nature-man is re-established" (*The Home of Man*, 1941).

33. The Radiant Farm, 1934. "It is something very like a *natural* event. Something like the humanized face of the land itself. A sort of geometrical plant as profoundly linked to the landscape as a tree or a hill, and as expressive of our human presence as a piece of furniture or a machine...." (*The Radiant City*).

"THE FARMHOUSE—Standardized and mass-produced construction susceptible of varying combinations. Under the house: stairs down to cellar, laundry, garbage chute from kitchen. The gallery is on the axis of the farm. The flower garden is in front of it, on the way to the kitchen garden and poultry yard" (*The Radiant City*).

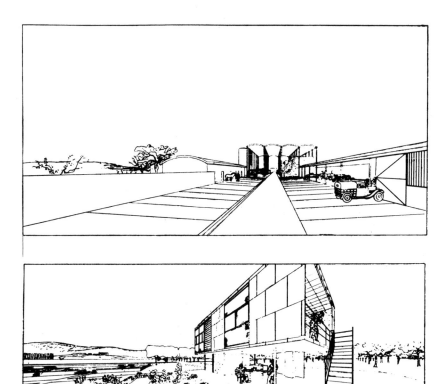

34. The Radiant Village, 1934–38. *Above:* Plan. 1. Silo. 2. Workshops. 3. Cooperative. 4. School. 5. Post and telegraph office. 6. Apartment house. 7. Club. 8. Town Hall. *Below:* Model.

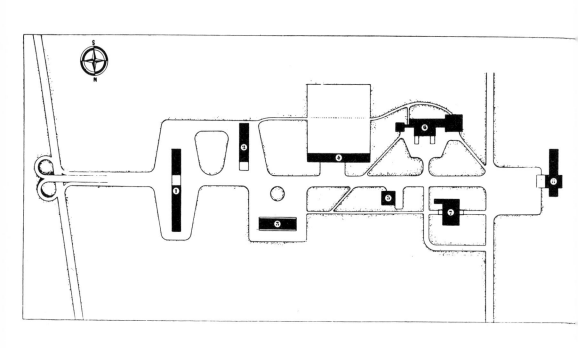

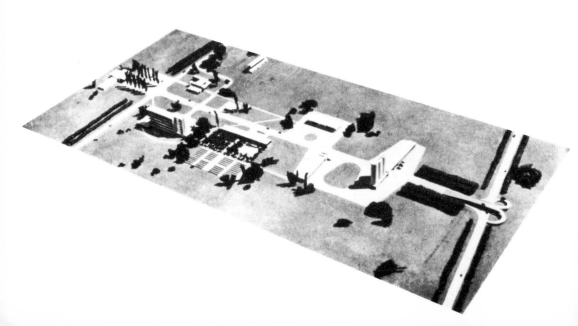

35. The C.I.A.M. grid, 1947. The grid was a procedure for the organization and display of city planning material developed by A.S.C.O.R.A.L., the French section of C.I.A.M. Information was coordinated in terms of dwelling, work, cultivation of mind and body, and circulation, with parallel presentations grouped under headings of the environment site planning, built volume, equipment, ethics and aesthetics, social and economic factors, legislation and steps in realization.

Above: Model of C.I.A.M. grid.
Center left: Model of typical plate.
Center right and Below: Examples of packaging and presentation.

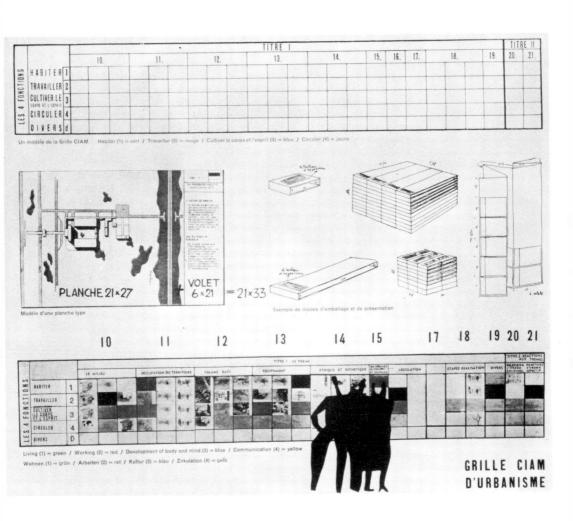

36. Scheme proposed in 1933 to develop the left bank of the Schelde in Antwerp according to the principles of the Radiant City.
37. Detail of the Antwerp scheme showing the principal avenue flanked by apartment housing and high-rise commercial building.

38. Plan for Nemours (Jamad-el-Ghazuat) in Algeria, projected in 1934. A. Residential district of high-rise housing, with area for extension. B. District of single-family houses. C. Native quarter. D. Civic center. E. Tourist center. F. Stadium. G. Business district and railway station. H. Industrial district. I. Gas and electricity. K. Port and fishing industry. M. Military base. O. Schools. P. Beach. R. Hospital.

39. The site of Nemours sketched by Le Corbusier.

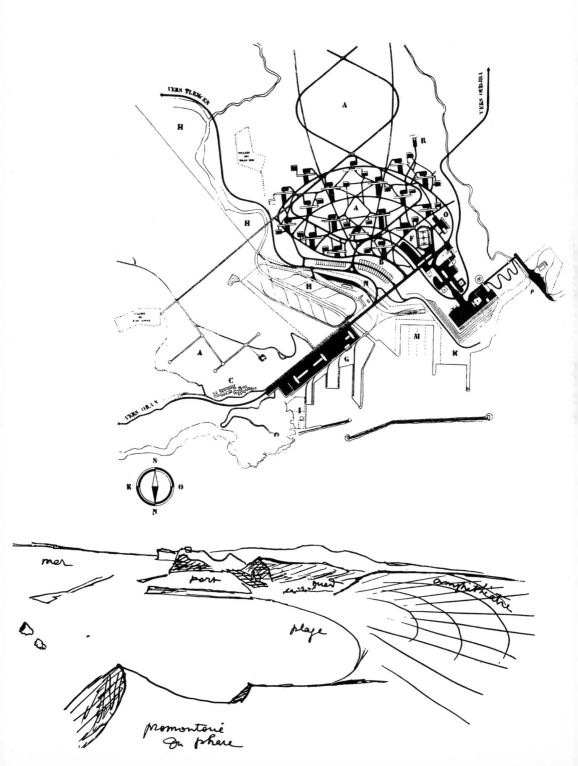

40. Sketch of Montevideo, 1929, containing a projected motor freeway that is combined with an apartment building which juts out over the water.
41. Sketch plan for São Paulo, 1929, proposing cross axes of elevated freeways containing apartment housing below the roadway.

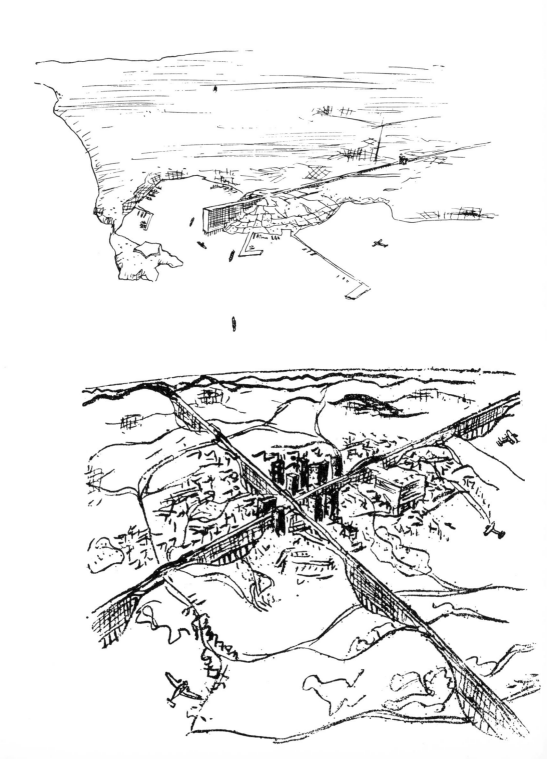

42. Rio de Janeiro, 1929. "This sketch, done in the plane: an idea is born" (*The Radiant City*, 1935).

43. "Rio de Janeiro: Paradise of tumultuous forms rising amid tropical vegetation. The Urbanist is conquered by the topography... until now. But the Urbanist is saved by the topography if he calls on the miracle of modern techniques... and on his creative lyricism. Now this site, wild, intractable, is grasped by the hand of man. And in an ineffable symphony, nature and geometry harmonize in a sculptural poem"—author's translation (*Le Lyrisme des temps nouveaux et l'Urbanisme*, 1939).

44. Plan for the redevelopment of Buenos Aires based on studies initiated in 1929. New port facilities are included, together with establishment of a commercial center projecting into the Rio de la Plata. A. Airport and terminal. B. Industrial port. C. Commercial area. D. Commercial port.

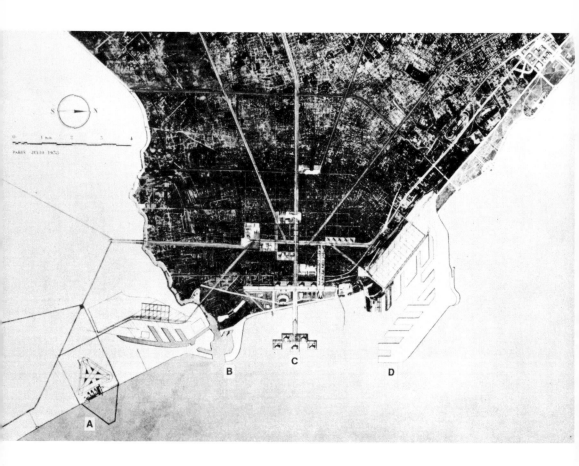

45. Project A for Algiers, 1930. An elevated motor freeway containing housing below the road level follows the coastline to the center of the city. An elevated site, Fort l'Empereur, is similarly developed with curving apartment slabs. "Why these curving forms at Fort l'Empereur? 1. To view broad horizons in all directions; 2. to respond to the landscape's invitation, an event of plastic creativity: response to horizons carries further; response to winds and sun is truer. A lyrical event" (*The Radiant City*).

46. Le Corbusier's scheme for Algiers, showing the plan of the elevated roadways.

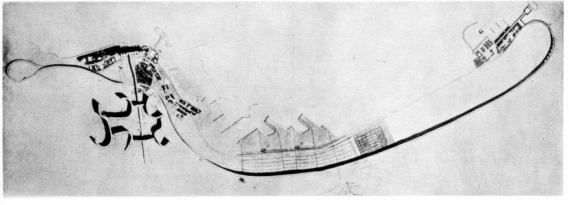

47. "Artificial sites" created underneath the elevated freeway, to be built according to the owner's predilections. Algiers, 1930.

48. "People of Algiers! Here we are on the highway, elevation 100 meters, driving along at top speed, looking out over a landscape that is sublime (because *we see it, having conquered it, having constructed it*). I am not deluding myself; but I say to you, people of Algiers, citizens of Algiers that, having erected this city of Modern Times for all the world to see, you would be proud, and happy!" (*The Radiant City*).

49. Algiers Project B, 1933, showing Le Corbusier's proposed elevated roadways and high-rise waterfront business center.

50. Algiers plan, 1942. 1. Apartment housing. 2. Circuit road giving access to the heights. 3. Small industry below the cliff. 4. Skyscraper business center. 5. Port. 6. Civic center facing the sea. 7. Moslem institutions. 8. Peninsula of the Admiralty. 9. The Casbah. 10. Limit of extension for the city. 12. Heavy industry at a distance from the city. 13. Weekend resort.

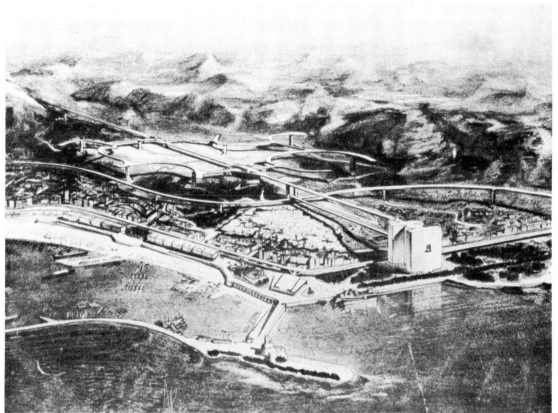

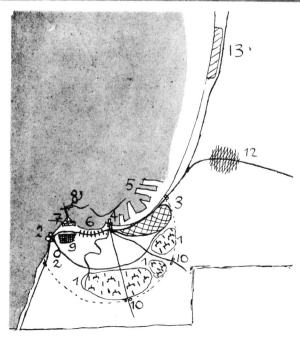

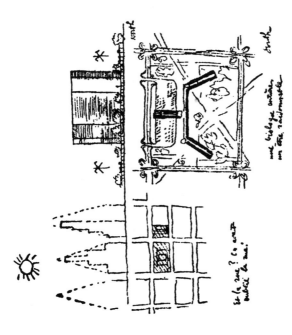

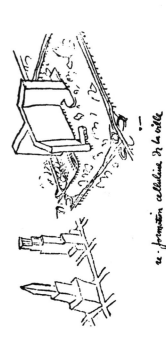

51. Sketches by Le Corbusier contrasting the New York skyscrapers with his own schematic design (*When the Cathedrals Were White*, 1937).

52. Sketches of New York, 1935. "The first shows New York up to 1900—like any traditional town before the arrival of mechanical means of transport. The second up to 1935—the modern city—the achievement of height. The skyscrapers are too small and houses still cluster round their bases. The crisis of today is the result of having superimposed the modern city on a framework surviving from the pre-machine age. The third transformation involves a programme of vast undertakings—undertakings well thought out and to the scale of our time" (*Oeuvre complète 1934–38*).

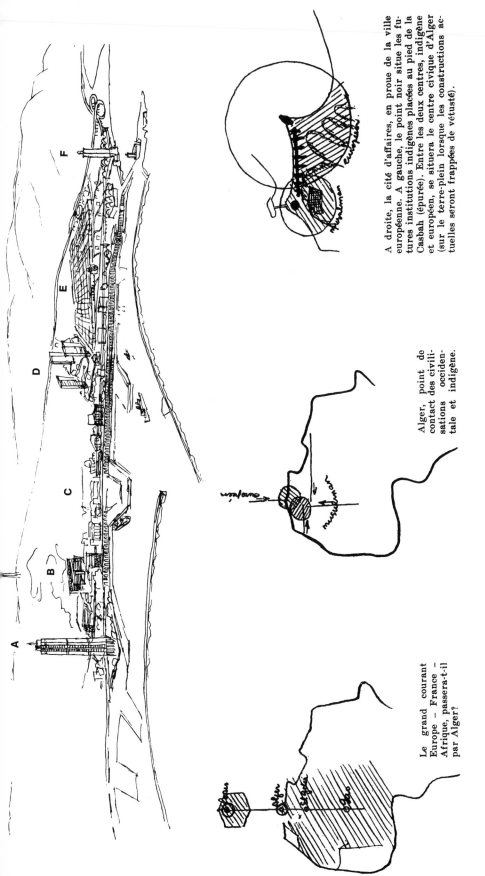

A droite, la cité d'affaires, en proue de la ville européenne. A gauche, le point noir situe les futures institutions indigènes placées au pied de la Casbah (épurée). Entre les deux centres, indigène et européen, se situera le centre civique d'Alger (sur le terre-plein lorsque les constructions actuelles seront frappées de vétusté).

Alger, point de contact des civilisations occidentale et indigène.

Le grand courant Europe – France – Afrique, passera-t-il par Alger?

53. View of Algiers showing proposals of the 1942 plan. A. Business center. B. Civic center. C. Port. D. Site of future apartment houses. E. The Casbah. F. Moslem institutions in the marine quarter.

54. The 1942 master plan for Algiers. Le Corbusier envisioned the city in terms of a meeting of two cultures, the Moslem and the European.

55. Sketches by Le Corbusier of the Casbah in Algiers. "Arab urbanism: excellent. Recognition of the constituent elements of the natural setting. Precise standards of protection and organization" (*Manière de penser sur l'urbanisme*).

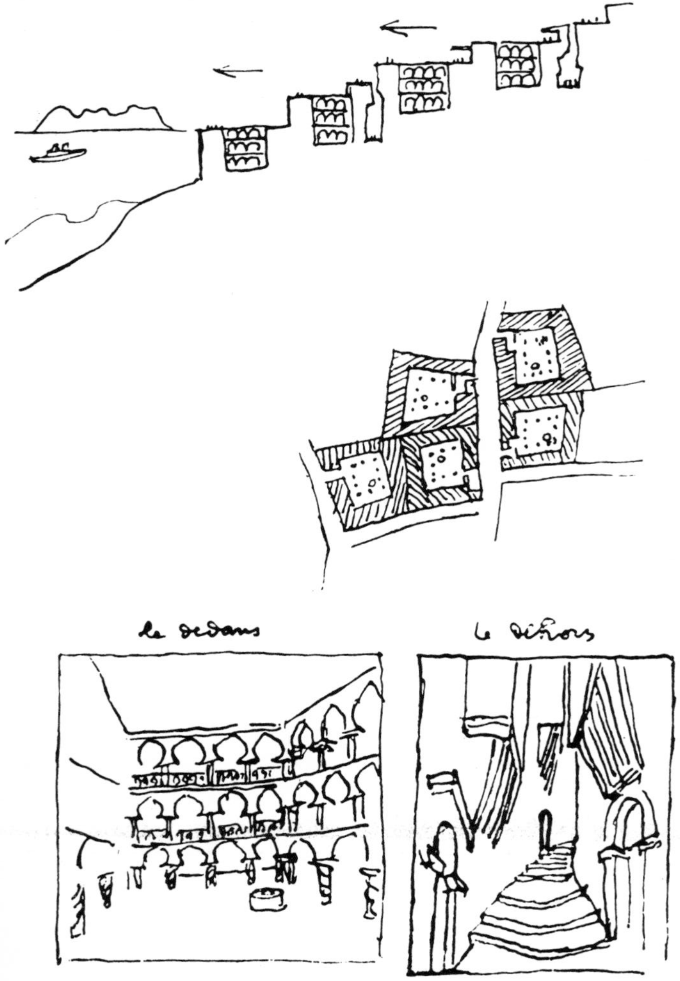

URBANISME ARABE) : excellent

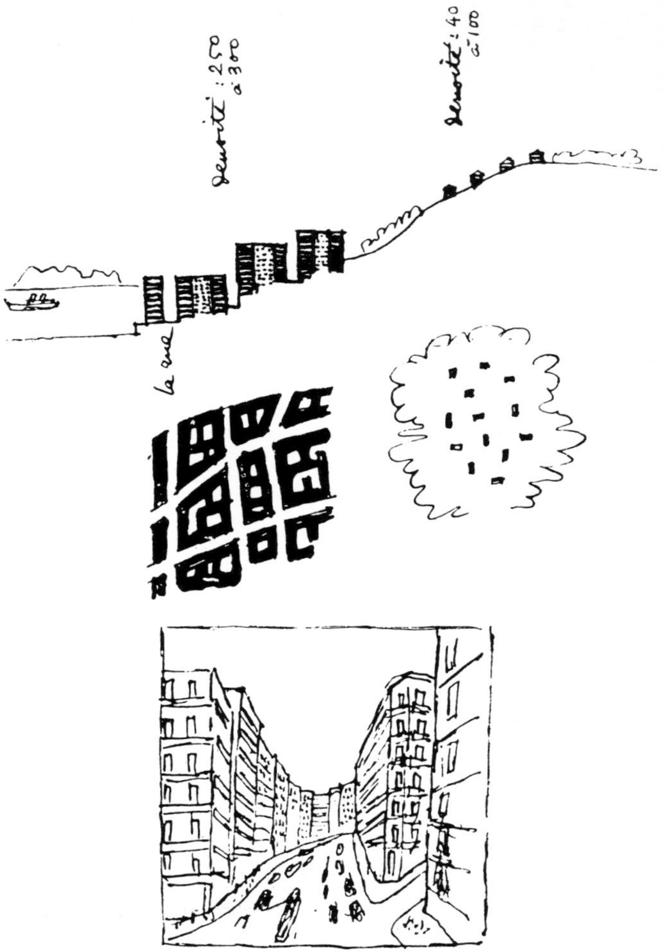

la rue

le piétons

(URBANISME EUROPEEN) : néfaste
MESURES D'INTERDICTION FRAPPANT
DEUX USAGES NEFASTES :

56. Sketches of the French section of Algiers. "European urbanism: baneful. Building regulations produce two ill-fated usages: a. The city block built on streets and courts;

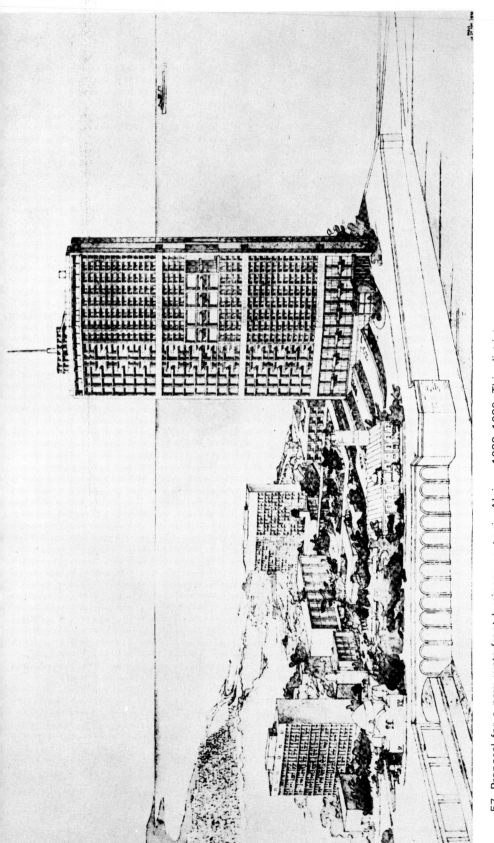

57. Proposal for a new waterfront business center in Algiers, 1938–1939. This district would form part of the 1942 master plan.

58. The Three Human Establishments, 1942–43.
A pattern of regional settlement combining
radio-concentric cities, linear-industrial settlements, and farming units.

59. Le Corbusier's conception of an overall pattern
of linear urban development for Europe.
"Society is spread over all the surface of the
earth, from one pole to the other, and including
the poles, a world composed of veins, of
gigantic forces of production, of gigantic
means of circulation and transport .... this is
no more, for the moment, than a stroke of
pencil across the map. It will be incumbent on
others, one day, to discover the true line"—
author's translation (*Oeuvre complète 1938–
46*). The letters mark ports or interchanges:
Bordeaux, La Rochelle, Nantes, Le Havre,
Rotterdam, Hamburg, Königsburg, Moscow,
Odessa, Salonika, Trieste.

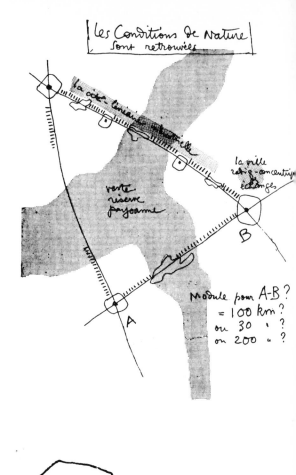

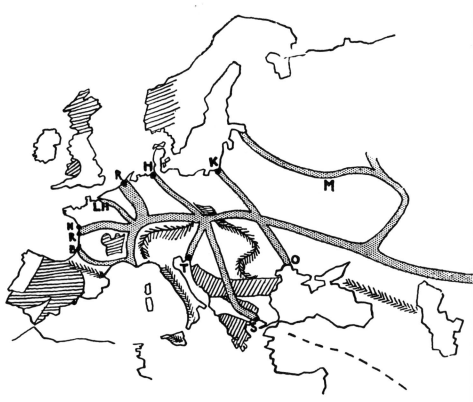

60. Schematic diagram of the linear-industrial city, c. 1942. Radio-concentric cities of more traditional formation would continue as centers of government and commercial exchange, linked together by a pattern of industrial-urban development following major lines of transport. Factory complexes would lie adjacent to rail, motor, and water transportation, while residential communities would be sited parallel to the industrial area, separated by a greenbelt containing a motor freeway.

61. Detail of a linear-industrial complex. A. Single-family houses. B. Apartment housing. C. Access road to the factory. D. Road connecting housing and community facilities. E. Pedestrian pathway. F. Greenbelt separating factories and housing, containing motor freeway. G. Area of community services (schools, cinemas, sports facilities, etc.). H. Factory. I. Transport lines (rail, water, motor).

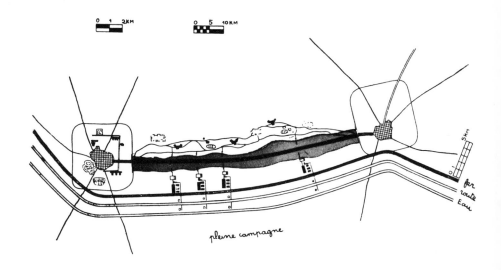

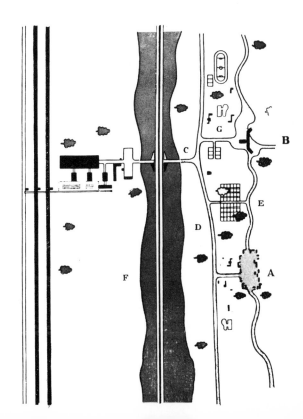

62. A "green factory" (*l'Usine-Verte*) projected for a linear-industrial city.

63. Diagram of a "unit of agricultural exploitation," showing individual farms, cooperative center, and highway.

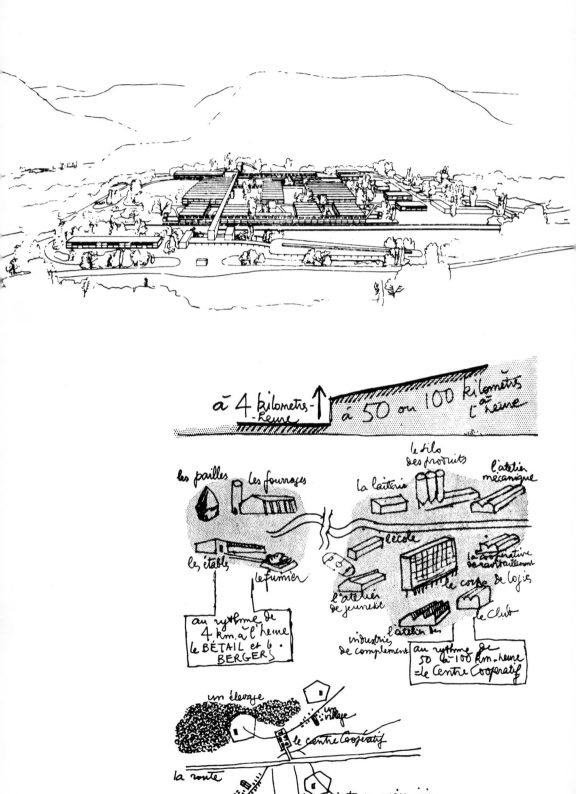

64. The civic center of Saint Dié as projected in 1946.
65. Plan of the Saint Dié civic center. 1. Administrative center. 2. Tourist and craft center. 3. Cafés. 4. Community center. 5. Museum. 6. Hotel. 7. Department stores. 8. Residential units to be erected immediately. 9. Factories. 10. Swimming pools.

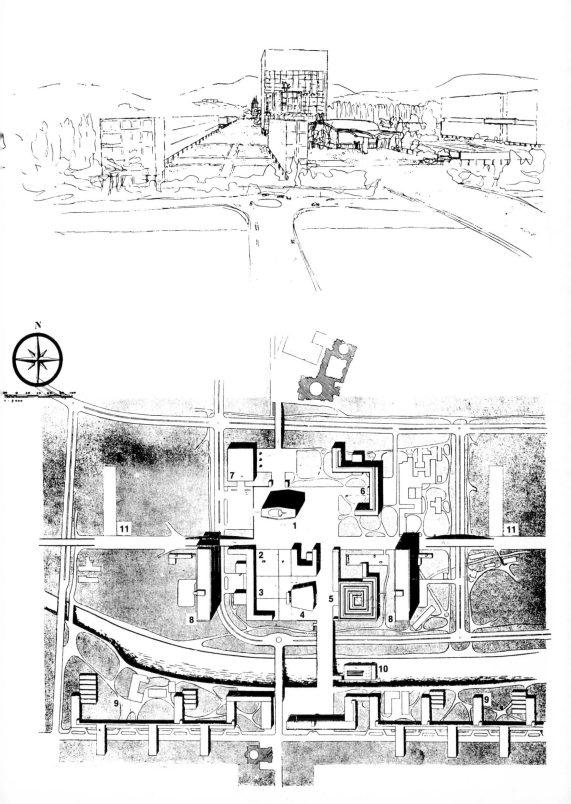

66. A district of South Marseilles with proposed Unité d'Habitation housing. Only the apartment house at left center was actually constructed.

67. For the Marseilles scheme, Le Corbusier initiated a system of traffic separation which he termed "the 7V's" (*les Sept Voies*), shown here in diagrammatic form. The V1 represented a regional road, the V2 a major urban artery, and the V3 a motor road surrounding residential sectors. The V4 would form a shopping street, while the V5 and V6 streets would provide access to individual dwellings. (The V6 was also conceived as an "interior street" or apartment house corridor.) The V7, sited within parkland, would give pedestrian circulation to schools, clubs, and sport grounds. Adaptations of the 7V system were employed in the Bogotá plan and in Chandigarh.

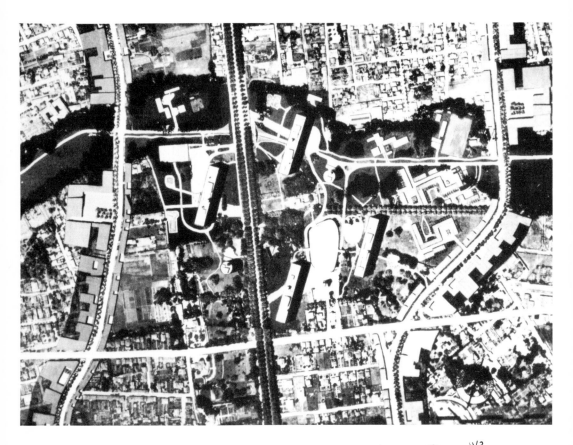

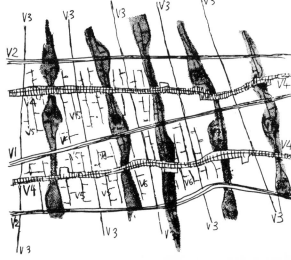

68. A grouping of apartment houses projected for Marseilles in 1945. Each building block, or Unité d'Habitation, would include within it communal facilities for shopping, sport, and child care.

69. The Unité d'Habitation at Marseilles, 1947–1952. (The small black rectangular patch represents 360 dwellings with communal services; the extensive white area represents 360 dwellings in the form of individual houses) (*Creation is a Patient Search*, 1960).

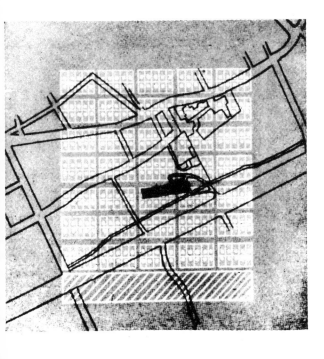

70. Section showing typical apartments in the Unité d'Habitation. This type of dwelling unit, containing a two-story living room, had evolved from Le Corbusier's "freehold maisonette" apartments (*Immeubles-Villas*) of the 1920's and from the design of the Radiant City. Each apartment extends through the width of the building, corridor access occurring on alternate floors.

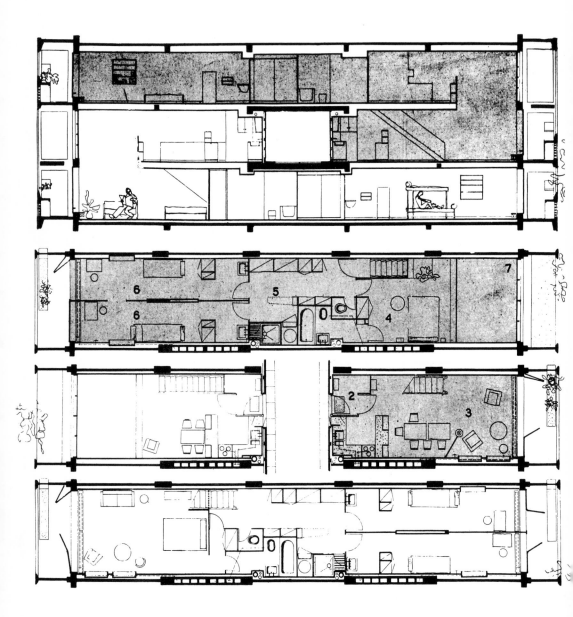

71. Le Corbusier liked to describe the apartment units of the Unité as fitting within the structural frame of the building like bottles in a rack.

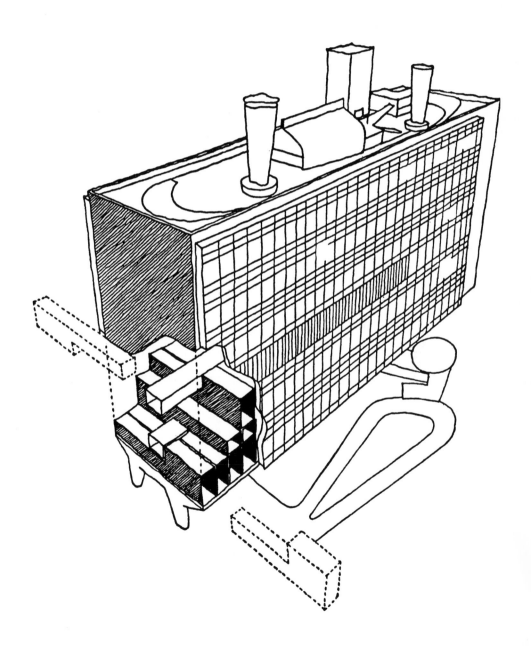

72. The Unité conception together with the 7V system shown in an unbuilt project for the town of Meaux, 1956–1957.

"Erection of five 'Housing Units of Proportioned Size (Unités d'Habitation...).' This scheme represents six years of preparatory work. Patience, therefore, is essential. Here will be found separate traffic ways for cars and pedestrians, as well as provision for 'individual-collectivity' (schools, clubs, parking places, repair shops for cars and bicycles, swimming pools, 'recreation at one's door step,' an infants' school on the roof, provision stores in each 'Unité' half-way up). Two towers, providing accommodation for single people and a hotel, are important additions to the life of the community. A 'V4' serves buildings offering amenities and essential services: the Civic Center, cinema, library, social insurance, post offices, fire station, police, business offices, cafés, etc.... The ten thousand inhabitants, thus comfortably established, are directly linked by 'V3s' and 'V8s' with the 'Linear Industrial Center,' which will be set up in the neighborhood" (*Creation is a Patient Search*).

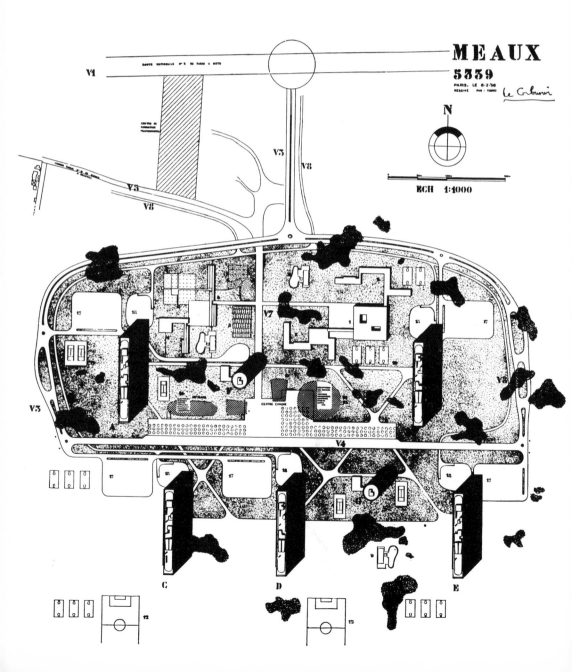

73. Pilot plan for the civic center of Bogotá proposed by Le Corbusier in 1950. A system of traffic separation is included, with through motor traffic restricted to the periphery, controlled vehicular access to buildings, and an internal network of pedestrian circulation. The historic center (G) would be limited to pedestrians, combining new construction with existing monuments, while an existing commercial street (C) would become a pedestrian promenade linking the district with a cultural center at left. Surrounding areas (H) would contain apartment housing.

74. Schematic plan of the residential superblock proposed for Bogotá. Each 800 × 1200 meter sector would contain an area of parkland providing sites for schools and community facilities. The 7V system of traffic separation is incorporated, employing a grid of major and minor streets.

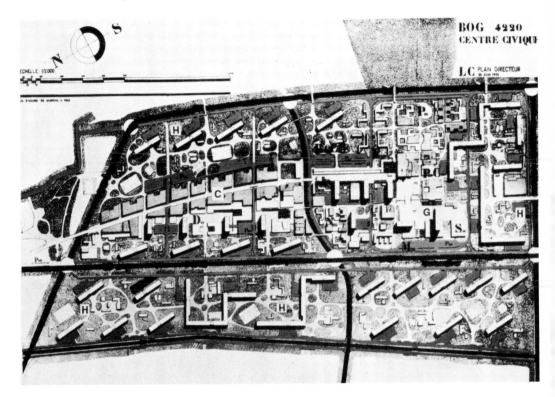

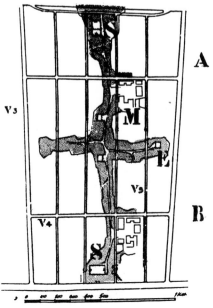

75. Master plan for Chandigarh completed in 1950 by Albert Mayer. Shaded portion indicates the area of initial development, while lower portion outlines the projected area of eventual expansion. White areas within shaded superblocks are internal parkland. Capitol complex is at upper edge of city. Central business district occupies superblock indicated by black square, and industrial area is indicated at right with crosshatching.

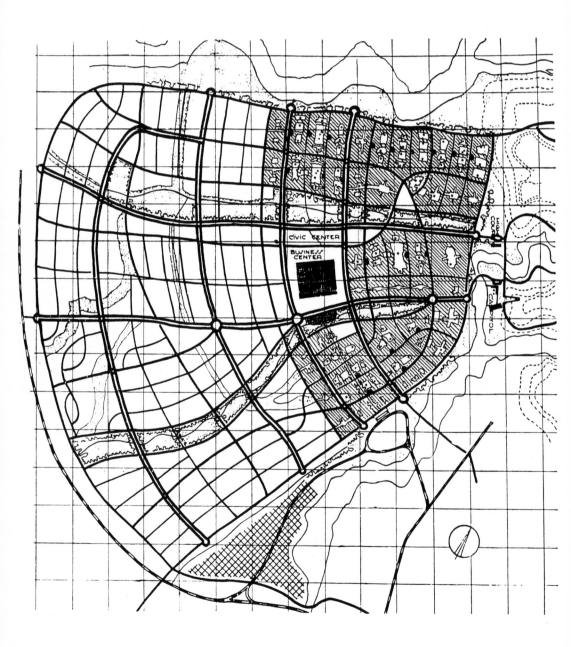

76. Schematic design for a typical three-block district in the Mayer plan. Housing areas are
    established on the periphery of the superblocks, with parkland in the center. Schools
    are sited in the parks, with bazaar areas at lower edges of blocks.

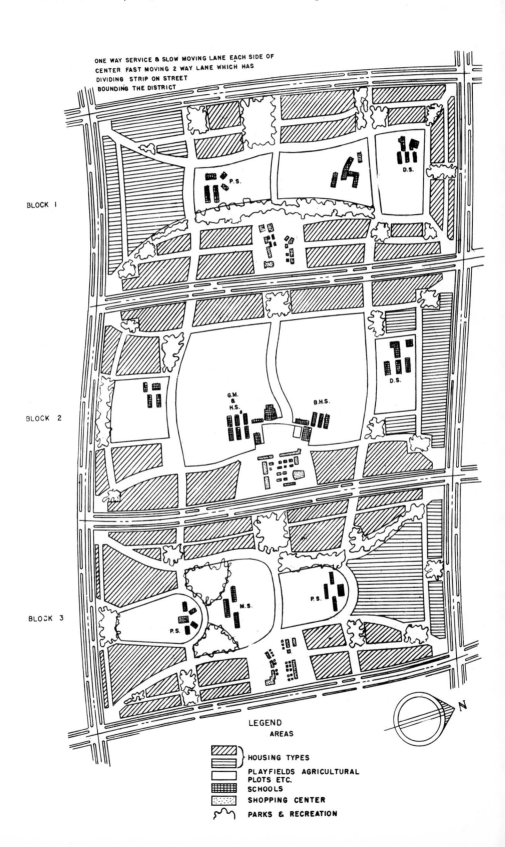

77–79. Studies for Chandigarh by Le Corbusier, 1951. The geometricized plan embodies a cross axis of major streets, and rectilinear 800 × 1200 meter residential sectors. The capitol complex is at the outer edge of the city, linked to the center by a monumental boulevard.

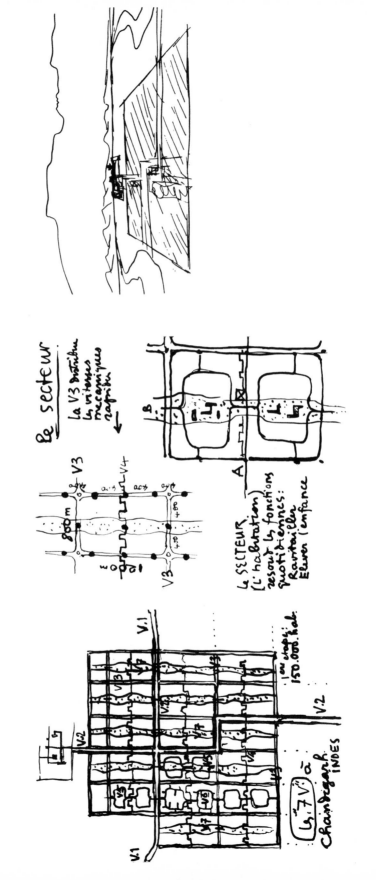

77. Schematic design of the residential sector. Each sector would be surrounded by streets carrying through traffic (V3), and bisected by a neighborhood shopping street (V4 and A). Loop roads would distribute local traffic, while a band of parkland (B) would extend

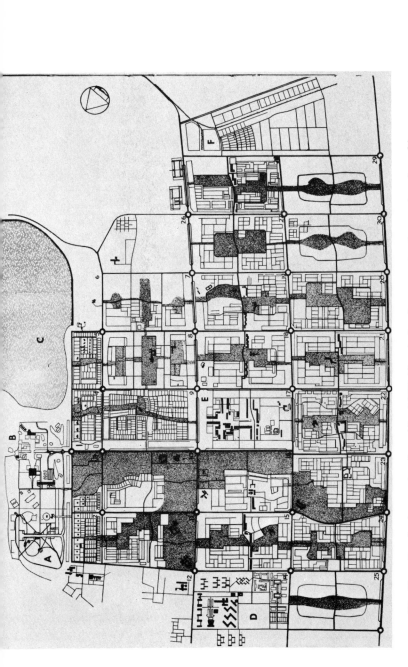

80. Chandigarh plan as developed by 1962. The design incorporates the master plan of Le Corbusier with detailed sector layouts by the Capital Project Office. Le Corbusier's 7V system of traffic separation provides a large-scale grid in which rapid motor vehicles are restricted to the V3 streets surrounding the residential sectors, while a variety of irregular streets serves the needs of local traffic. Each sector is bisected by a V4 shopping street which, in turn, is intersected by a loop road, the V5, serving as the principal internal distributor. A central band of parkland containing V7 pedestrian paths is provided within each sector. A. Rajendra Park (a recreational area adjacent to the capitol complex. B. Capitol complex). C. Lake (an artificial lake created by damming a riverbed adjacent to the site). D. University (Sector 14). E. Central business district and civic center (Sector 17). F. Industrial area.

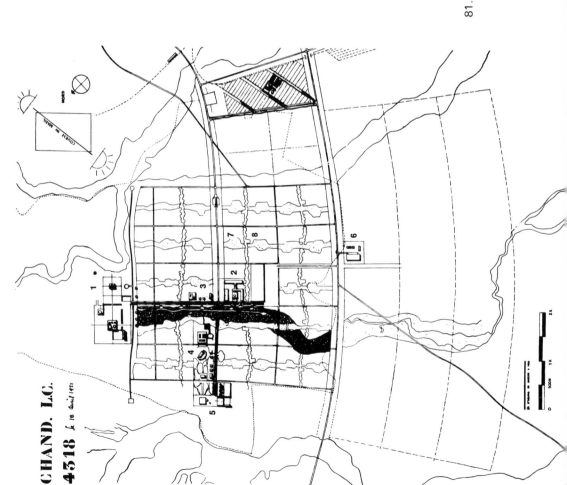

81. Le Corbusier's master plan for Chandigarh, dated April 18, 1951. 1. Capitol complex. 2. Central business district. 3. Hotels, restaurants, and visitors' center. 4. Museums and stadium. 5. University. 6. Wholesale market. 7. Park bands extending through residential sectors. 8. Shopping street (V4). 9. The area below the market would contain future extensions of the city to a total population of 500,000.

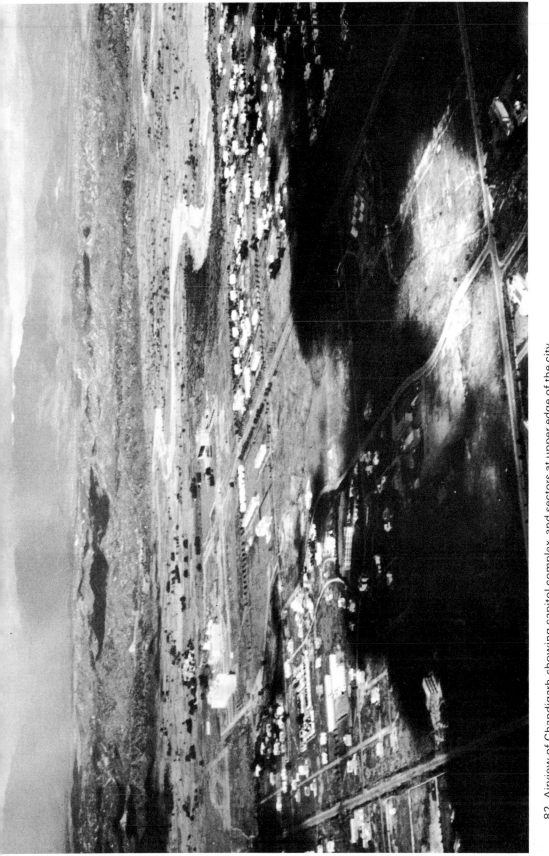

82. Airview of Chandigarh showing capitol complex and sectors at upper edge of the city.

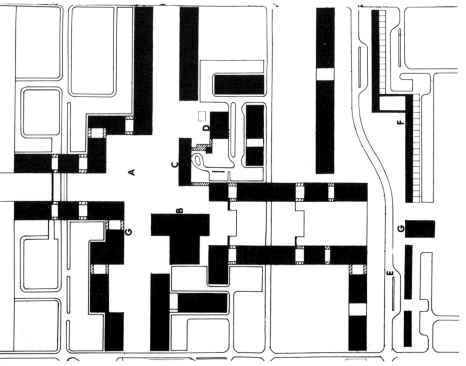

83. Plan of central business district occupying Sector 17 north of the V4 bazaar street. A. Main square or *Chowk*. B. Ten-story building. C. Town hall. D. State library of Punjab. E. V4 bazaar street. F. Shops. G. Cinemas.

84. Central business district. State Library of Punjab at left and State Bank of India at right

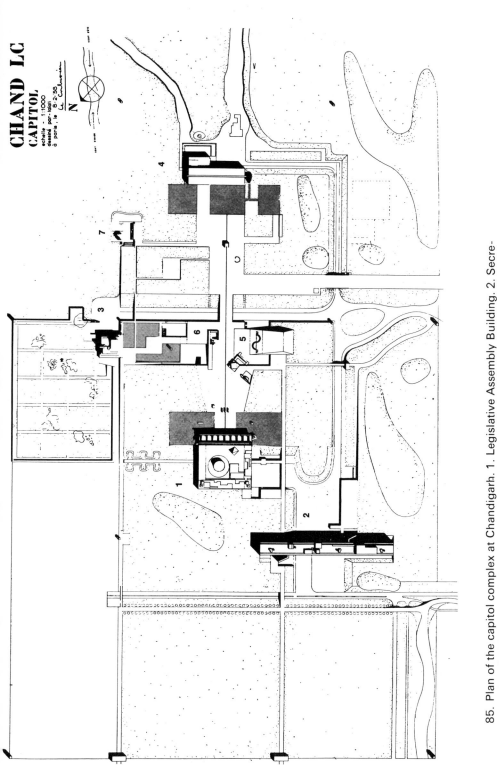

85. Plan of the capitol complex at Chandigarh. 1. Legislative Assembly Building. 2. Secretariat. 3. Museum of Knowledge (formerly site of the Governor's Palace). 4. High Court. 5. Monument of the Twenty-four Solar Hours and Tower of Shade. 6. Martyrs' Monument (a monument to the martyrs of the Punjab partition). 7. Monument of the Open Hand.

86. The Secretariat and Legislative Assembly seen from the High Court.
87. The High Court seen from the excavated parking lot of the Legislative Assembly. In the foreground is a covered passageway leading from the Secretariat.

89. The approach to the Governor's Palace as initially projected for the capitol complex, 1952.

90. Studies for the monuments of Chandigarh, 1952. Top: The Twenty-four Solar Hours. Center: The Modulor and Harmonic Spiral, and a structure illustrating the pattern of the two yearly solstices. Bottom: The Tower of Shade (a demonstration of architectural sun control), and the Open Hand.

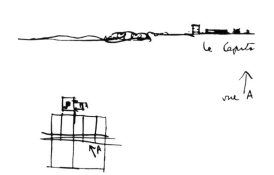

94. Photomontage showing the projected Monument of the Open Hand standing at the outer edge of the capitol complex.

95. The Legislative Assembly in Chandigarh. The monumental portico faces the central esplanade of the government complex.

96. The Chandigarh Secretariat with the Assembly portico at right.
97. The entrance façade of the High Court in Chandigarh. The portico was subsequently polychromed.

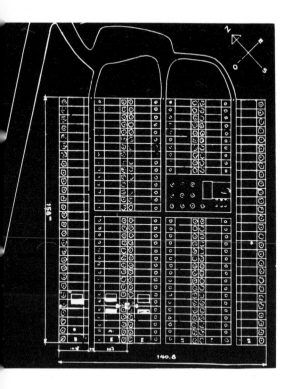

Le Corbusier's only contribution to the design of housing in Chandigarh lay in a study for prototypical low-cost housing. He proposed that small row houses be grouped together in "villages" of 184 houses (750 inhabitants). "It will be admitted that 1 200 square feet [111. 6 square meters] between four walls can make a home. Sun, space, greenery, part covered, part open in shade, and part completely in the open air with the inevitable variety of the nearby street. By placing all the families side by side, they are completely separated and have absolute privacy. It is the same principle which was employed in the large apartment blocks.... A group of 750 inhabitants forms a village, the roads become interior corridors of clean bricks on which one walks barefoot. Motor vehicles and drawn carts must stay outside the square (about 23,400 square yards) which forms the unit called 'a village'" (*Oeuvre complète 1946–52*). A similar "village" grouping was subsequently adapted in Chandigarh for some types of housing.

98. "Village" layout.

99. Plans and cross sections of houses. 1. Veranda. 2. Parents' room. 3. Children's room. 4. Kitchen. 5. Toilet. 6. Shower. 7. Brise soleil. 8. Parasol roof.

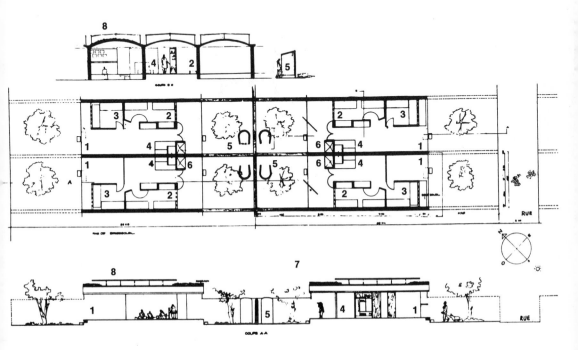

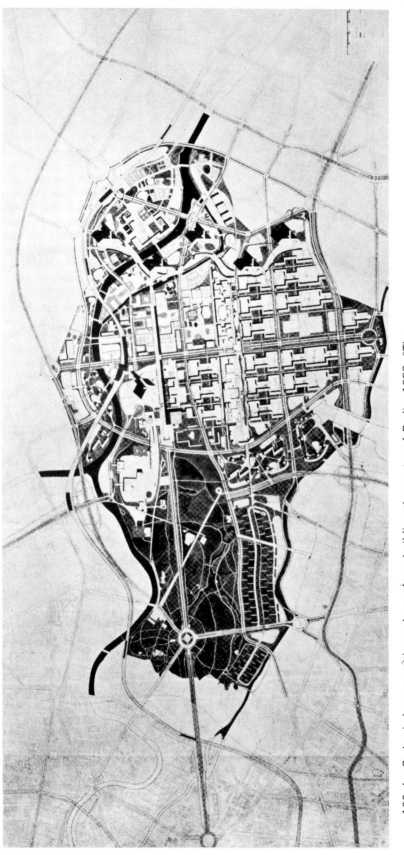

100. Le Corbusier's competition scheme for rebuilding the center of Berlin, 1958. "The Crime? Le Corbusier had provided in his plan that the Avenue 'Unter den Linden' be reserved exclusively for pedestrians (shown in white on the plan). Automobile traffic was channeled across at intervals by means of elevated highways leading down to parking places right in front of the buildings—multi-level parking. The Avenue 'Unter den Linden' would have become the grand promenade, modern this time. In previous times it had been the avenue for walkers (before the automobile). But the jury decreed that the 'Linden' be covered with automobiles as in all the rest of the world" (*Oeuvre complète 1957–65*).

N

101. Lucio Costa, planner: Plan of Brasilia, 1956.

102. Motor axis and residential superblocks of Brasilia.

at Nantes (1952–1953), one at Briey-en-Forêt (1957), and the third in Berlin (1956–1958).

In 1950, Le Corbusier formulated a pilot plan for Bogotá, from which a master plan was developed by José Luis Sert and Paul Lester Wiener (*Fig. 73*). This scheme included redevelopment of the civic center, the establishment of new transportation arteries, and a residential system of 800 x 1,200 meter superblocks serving as neighborhood units (*Fig. 74*). Although initially granted official approval, the plan was subsequently hampered in execution through changes in political administration.

Thus, although Europe, and much of the rest of the world, was entering a period of rapid rebuilding and increasing urbanization, Le Corbusier seemed destined to continue his familiar path of frustration and rejection.

CHANDIGARH

In spite of his fame as a theoretical urban designer, Le Corbusier might well have concluded his career without ever participating directly in a successful urban plan were it not for two gentlemen from India who, in November, 1950, approached him with regard to the development of a new capital for the province of Punjab. Although the proposal seemed in many ways unpromising, Le Corbusier, after some hesitation, agreed to join the project, and the remote provincial town of Chandigarh now remains his only realized plan.

Le Corbusier was engaged primarily as an architect, rather than as a planner. A master plan for the Punjab capital had already been designed by the New York firm of Mayer, Whittlesey and Glass (*Figs. 75–76*), and Le Corbusier's services were sought for the architectural realization of this scheme. It was natural, however, in view of his long involvement with urban design, that Le Corbusier would seek to modify the existing plan somewhat when he began its execution (*Figs. 80–81*).

Le Corbusier was the dominant member of a group of designers engaged in Chandigarh, including his cousin, Pierre Jeanneret, and the British architects Maxwell Fry and Jane Drew.[100] In the division of labor, Le Corbusier was to concentrate his efforts on the overall ordering of the master plan and the design of major architectural monuments, leaving the detailed development of the urban fabric, including housing design, to his colleagues.

Chandigarh had been conceived in a time of crisis following the partition of India, during which the province of Punjab had been divided, with the capital city of Lahore going to Pakistan. The decision to construct the new city was motivated partly by necessity, but represented also the desire to respond to political uncertainty with a symbolic gesture of strength and creativity. The colonial yoke had been discarded, and the opportunity had arrived for India to demonstrate that she could stand alone, that she could command her own destiny and govern her own house, and that against the brutality of nature and the vastness of her continent she could impress an ordered, yet viable pattern of human life. Viewing the new city as a focal point of national importance, Prime Minister Nehru had said, "Let this be a new town, symbolic of the freedom of India, unfettered by the traditions of the past... an expression of the nation's faith in the future."[101]

Although the Chandigarh project was meant to symbolize India's independence, a lack of trained local technicians had necessitated the importation of foreign planners. The plan as it had been developed by the Mayer firm represented in many ways a synthesis of Western urban design theory, incorporating a system of residential neighborhood units containing schools, housing, small commerce and parkland, a system of pedestrian and motor separation, and discrete zoning of major activities (cf. Figs. 75–76). At the upper edge of the city a complex of government buildings was projected, while a commercial district was sited toward the center, and an industrial area placed at one side.

The initial planners had to a degree been dominated by the Garden City predilection for low-density, somewhat picturesque design, and Le Corbusier, although retaining many general features of the original scheme, began his modifications by classicizing and geometricizing the plan, straightening major streets and transforming the slightly irregular superblocks into rectangles. He sought to give the city a large-scale unified design appropriate to its monumental character, establishing within the new rectilinear outlines a cross-axial configuration of major boulevards focusing on the commercial center, with the capitol complex culminating the northeastern axis toward the mountains (Figs. 77–82).

Referring to the Chandigarh project, Le Corbusier once stated, "I have conceived a capital for the Punjab, a completely new town, standing on a plain at the foot of the Himalaya. As architect I had a free hand but very little money.

"This gave great scope for ideas, invention and imagination. But the program provided by the authority is banal and unimaginative, both for the housing and for the institutional elements of the town. Nowhere yet have the fundamental problems of town planning been put, the problems of economy, sociology and ethics, the conquest of which will make man the master of his civilization."[102]

In addition to whatever programmatic limitations the project embodied, Chandigarh also presented Le Corbusier with a set of technical and social conditions far removed from the industrialized society for which he had always projected his schemes. The means for large-scale mechanized transport did not exist; a shortage of steel coupled with inadequate technical services made high-rise building unfeasible, while the climate and semirural way of life mitigated against apartment housing.

Although plunged into an unfamiliar environment, and compelled to work in conditions unfavorable to his previous predilections, Le Corbusier found in India perhaps the most receptive patronage he had ever known. His unwavering confidence was reassuring to the Indians, while the largeness of his vision and the grandness of his concepts seemed to harmonize appropriately with their aspirations for the new capital. Although he had frequently found government officials less than sympathetic, his personal relations with the Indian administrators of Chandigarh seem altogether successful; and Prime Minister Nehru, who took great interest in the project, became a warm friend. It was once observed that "India understands idea men and treats them well—perhaps better than any other country—and Le Corbusier benefits from this."[103]

After a lifetime of seeking to master the demands of the machine age, Le Corbusier found himself trying to come to terms with an environment still largely untouched by industrialism. Describing his Indian experience, he once wrote: "In modern life, today so distracting, Le Corbusier finds in India a friendly terrain: this old tradition where man is face to face with nature, with her violence also. Friendly contacts with nature, the animals, the creatures, sleeping under the stars, a land far removed from the stupidity of certain comforts ... so often questionable. Le Corbusier has found in this land the opportunity to apply all his energy in the search for solutions which surpass ordinary architecture. It concerns a truly human problem freed of all conformity."[104]

In general, the conception of Chandigarh represented a relaxation of the rigid geometry which had dominated Le Corbusier's earlier designs, embodying an interweaving of geometric and picturesquely ordered elements. The determination of proportions in the civic design as well as in the architecture involved use of the Modulor, a system of proportioning which he had evolved during World War II and patented as an invention in 1947, but related also to traditional classical ordering. The basic unit of the city, the residential sector, was formed on the golden rectangle, with dimensions of 800 x 1,200 meters (1/2 x 3/4 miles).[105]

The measurement of 800 meters, which recurs in the planning of the capitol complex and elsewhere, may be found also in the monumental composition which Le Corbusier admired in his native Paris. In Paris, it is 800 meters from the Louvre to the Place de la Concorde, and another 800 meters from the Place de la Concorde to the Place Clemenceau, while the Madeleine and the Chambre des Députés terminate opposite ends of an 800-meter axis passing through the Place de la Concorde. In Chandigarh, the distance along the monumental avenue between the commercial center and the capitol complex duplicates that between the Étoile and the Place de la Concorde. Although it is not unnatural that Le

Corbusier, in ordering a totally new urban pattern, might be inspired by the dimensions of a familiar and beloved city, the monumental effectiveness of the Indian capital may be vitiated through lack of a correspondingly scaled urban architecture.

In developing the plan of Chandigarh, Le Corbusier employed a scheme of traffic separation which he termed "the 7V's" (*les Sept Voies*), a system which he had previously projected for Bogotá (*Figs. 73–74*) and South Marseilles (*Fig. 67*). Some degree of traffic separation had always been present in Le Corbusier's schemes, and the 7V's represented an attempt to develop a fully organized, universally applicable system dividing traffic into a series of seven categories comprising a hierarchy of circulation ranging from arterial roads to apartment house corridors (*Figs. 77–79*).

The specific organization of the 7V system in Chandigarh is as follows: The V1 represents regional roads leading into the city from the outside, while the V2 designation refers to the two major cross-axial boulevards of the city. One of these provides the ceremonial avenue linking the central district with the capitol complex, while the other forms a cultural-commercial axis. Surrounding the residential sectors and establishing the gird pattern of the city are the V3 streets intended for fast motor traffic. Frontage development along these streets is prohibited, the sectors being designed to focus inwardly. Bisecting the long side of each sector is a bazaar street—the V4—following a slightly irregular path and permitting a variety of slow-moving traffic. This street, intended to provide for neighborhood shopping needs, carries shops only on the south side, to ensure shade for pedestrians and also to eliminate excessive street crossing. The V5 is a loop road intersecting the V4 and serving as the main distributor of traffic within the sector, while V6 lanes give additional access to houses. A strip of parkland containing schools extends through each sector, providing continuous bands of open space throughout the city, and including the V7 pedestrian paths.[106]

Applying his favorite biological analogy to the road system, Le Corbusier stated, "The 7V's act in the town plan as the blood stream, the lymph system and the respiratory system act in biology. In biology these systems are quite rational, they are different from each other, there is no confusion between them, yet they are in harmony. They create order. It is God who has placed them in the world; it is for us to learn from them when we are organizing the ground which lies beneath our feet"[107] (*cf. Fig. 67*).

The abundant provisions for motor traffic in Chandigarh represented anticipation of future mechanization, rather than a system adapted to existing conditions, although the wide mixtures of traffic characteristic of Indian cities, ranging from trucks and automobiles to bicycles and bullock carts, justified an elaborate system of separation. The success of the Chandigarh system, however, can only be evaluated when traffic volumes, especially of motor traffic, have risen sufficiently to test the resources of the plan.

Both technical and social conditions determined that Chandigarh be predominantly a low-rise city, although in preliminary drawings, Le Corbusier indicated a desire for the inclusion of some high-rise building both in the capitol complex and the central business district. The architectural composition of the city reflected Le Corbusier's long-standing preference for a controlled environment—for a simplification of building types and a disciplined unity of building form. Government housing followed a pattern of standardized designs, while private housing was architecturally controlled. Neighborhood shops were built to specified designs, and in the central business district, a potentially competitive and varied architecture was forestalled by Le Corbusier's predetermined plan.

As ultimately developed by Le Corbusier, the central business district was architecturally unified by means of a standardized four-story, concrete frame building. Its height was determined by the lack of elevators— the size of building which most owners might be able to afford—and the possibility of earthquakes. Although interiors could be developed according to the builder's wishes, the exterior treatment was required to follow a prescribed design providing exterior verandas, that of the ground floor serving as a continuous 3.6-meter-wide pedestrian shelter (*Figs. 83–84*).

The largest building projected for the complex was a ten-story slab housing the post and telegraph building and providing the focal point of a central square (*Fig. 83*). Although the central business district was designed as a pedestrian area, with motor access restricted to the periphery, the dimensioning of circulation areas and open spaces seems excessive, and generally inappropriate both to the climate and the scale of the surrounding building. The design effort may have involved an attempt to balance the symbolically important capitol complex with another ensemble of monumental dimensions, but, lacking either symbolic purpose or compelling architecture, the business district may be deemed a questionable success both visually and functionally.

It was in the capitol complex, the symbolic focal point of the city, that Le Corbusier devoted his most intensive efforts (*Fig. 85*). This provincial government center, containing the High Court (*Fig. 87*), Legislative Assembly (*Fig. 88*), Secretariat (*Fig. 86*), and (initially) the Governor's Palace (*Fig. 89*), was sited at the upper edge of the city, surrounded by open land.

Within a stretch of open plain, in sight of the Himalayas which close the landscape to the north, Le Corbusier conceived a grandly scaled ensemble, basically ordered by a plan involving 800 and 400 meter squares, but depending for visual cohesion on an interplay of massive building forms seen against the distant mountains and within a configuration of excavated earth mounds and reflecting pools (*Fig. 88*). The scale of the complex is vast, in keeping with the surrounding landscape, an area designed for sweeping visual impact, rather than ease of physical communication. In designing this complex, Le Corbusier reported,

"There was anxiety and anguish in taking decisions on that vast, limitless ground. A pathetic soliloquy! I had to appreciate and to decide alone. The problem was no longer one of reasoning but of sensation. Chandigarh is not a city of lords, princes or kings confined within walls, crowded in by neighbors. It was a matter of occupying a plain. The geometrical event was, in truth, a sculpture of the intellect. ... It was a battle of space, fought within the mind. Arithmetic, texturique, geometrics: it would all be there when the whole was finished. For the moment, oxen, cows and goats, driven by peasants, crossed the sun-scorched fields"[108] (*Figs. 91–93*).

The capitol area as a whole was conceived as a pedestrian plaza, motor traffic being channeled into sunken trenches leading to parking areas (*Figs. 82, 85*). The generating motif of the complex was a slightly asymmetrical cross axis, one arm of which comprises a pedestrian promenade penetrating the area and extending the line of the monumental boulevard leading from the commercial center. The long slab of the Secretariat bounds the space to the left, and stands adjacent to the Legislative Assembly, while the High Court and Legislature terminate the cross axis on either side of a 450-meter esplanade. The center of the area is marked by a series of monuments (*Fig. 90*) devised to illustrate Le Corbusier's theories of city planning, while outlined against the hills at the outer edge of the complex was projected a Museum of Knowledge (on a set site originally for the Governor's Palace) and a symbolic sculptural monument designed by Le Corbusier in the form of a great open hand about 26 meters high (*Fig. 94*).

The monuments were reportedly suggested by Jane Drew who advised Le Corbusier to "set up in the heart of the Capitol the signs which symbolise the basis of your philosophy and by which you arrived at your understanding of the art of city design. These signs should be known—they are the key to the creation of Chandigarh."[109]

Included would be a symbolic representation of the Modulor and the Harmonic Spiral representing the Modulor series of proportions. Additional monuments were designed to represent the Twenty-four Solar Hours "which rule men's activity," and the path of the sun between two solstices, "this sun, which governs men—friend or enemy,"[110] while the Tower of Shade would demonstrate principles of sun protection. Near the approach to the Museum of Knowledge a monument was projected to the martyrs of the Indian partition. The Open Hand (*Fig. 94*)—sometimes referred to by the architect as the Monument of Chandigarh—was conceived by him in Paris in 1948 and "during the years that followed, it occupied my mind, finding its first existence in Chandigarh."[111] The symbolism, he claimed, arose "spontaneously, or more exactly, as the result of reflections and spiritual struggles arising from the feelings of anguish and disharmony which separate mankind, and so often create enemies. ... Little by little the open hand appeared as a possibility in great architectural compositions."[112]

Although some might question the suitability of including in the capitol complex what are in effect monuments to Le Corbusier himself, many have found their symbolism wholly appropriate. An Indian engineer wrote to Le Corbusier, "We have a word Ram Bharosa, which indicates deep faith in the ultimate—faith born of the surrender of the will to the Ultimate Source of Knowledge, service without reward and much more. I live in that faith and feel happy in the vision of the new city which is so safe and so secure in its creation in your hands. We are humble people. No guns to brandish, no atomic energy to kill. Your philosophy of 'open hand' will appeal to India and what we are taking from your open hand, I pray, may become a source of new inspiration in our architectural and city planning. We may on our side, when you come here next, be able to show you the spiritual heights to which some of the individuals have attained. Ours is a philosophy of open hand. Maybe Chandigarh becomes the new center of thought."[113]

Although some observers have been overwhelmed by the sweeping scale of the Chandigarh capitol complex, its architectural embodiment has been widely regarded as one of the most masterful achievements in modern building. Almost primordial in their evocative strength, the symbolic civic structures, through their massive plasticity of form, and bold use of exposed concrete, were influential in liberating postwar architecture from the formal restrictions of the International Style, reinforcing Le Corbusier's position as an innovative leader of modern design. For devotees of architecture, the Chandigarh capitol complex has become a place of pilgrimage, as much a part of the Indian itinerary as the Taj Mahal.

More importantly, Le Corbusier's efforts served to revitalize the modern concept of monumental building. Chandigarh was the product of political crisis, embodying the desire of a new nation, poor, technically undeveloped, and torn with inner dissension, to create a city symbolic of permanence and order, a focal point for the incipient nationalist spirit. As Le Corbusier had sought to redefine the master plan of the city to achieve a suitably monumental scale, so he struggled to give the capitol complex the imprint of unity and power appropriate to its symbolic function.

The Secretariat (*Fig. 96*), a long concrete slab, combines with the earth mounds to define the complex, becoming itself like a natural barrier—a man-made cliff providing a backdrop for the smaller structures. In keeping with its essentially utilitarian function, the Secretariat stands apart from the main plaza of the capitol upon which face the great entrance porticos of the High Court and Assembly buildings. Throughout the building ensemble is a subtle and harmonic interplay of diversity and unity: the High Court (*Fig. 97*) classically contained in outline, but split by a brilliantly painted portico, balanced by the Assembly (*Fig. 95*), its roofline pierced from within by the dramatically sculptural forms of the interior chambers, and carrying an external, free-standing portico like a giant brise soleil. The space of the plaza is vast, yet retains, albeit tenuously, a sense of place, partially enclosed by earth mounds, yet open to the mountains.

Although for much of his career, Le Corbusier's visionary architecture had symbolized a world of economic affluence, technical virtuosity, and mechanical comfort, he triumphantly culminated his career within a set of restraints both harsher and spiritually richer. As India herself stood alone and threatened when Chandigarh was planned, so the capitol structures seem to stand alone within a hostile world. They are not comfortable buildings, nor do they stand in a comfortable place. Nor do they speak of a comfortable life, or of a life taken for granted, but of a life maintained through effort and tenacity.

Disciplined by climate, poverty, and primitive technology, the buildings of the capitol complex rise from the earth, asserting the presence of man against the vast sweep of plain and the distant mountains. There is no shelter here. Battered by rains and dust storms, scorched by a brutal sun and buffeted by winds, these structures have been laboriously built by the toil of many men. They are meant to last. Like the classical builders he so admired, Le Corbusier countered the uncertainty of fate with a certainty of vision, establishing a bold and powerful testament for the future, whatever destiny it brings.

As he became more and more absorbed in the monumental architecture of Chandigarh, however, he tended to disassociate himself from the overall planning of the city, leaving primary responsibility for developing the urban design to the Capital Project Office directed by Pierre Jeanneret. During the years in which the city took form, Le Corbusier worked in Paris, visiting Chandigarh only periodically, while Pierre Jeanneret remained on the site directing construction as the Chief Architect and Planner of Punjab.

Le Corbusier's contribution to the design of the residential sectors consisted of a schematic outline providing a generalized pattern of street layout, parkland and bazaar placement. Within these sectors, the predominant visual character was determined by a prescribed program of thirteen categories of government housing, the initial housing-types having been developed by Maxwell Fry, Jane Drew, and Pierre Jeanneret. So significant is this hierarchic pattern of housing in the overall appearance of the city that there seem virtually to be two Chandigarhs, that of Le Corbusier embodied in the monumental foci, and that of Pierre Jeanneret comprising the bulk of the building (*Figs. 98–99*).

The master plan of Chandigarh (*Fig. 75*) implied the creation of a dual scale of urban design, a monumental scale allied to the capital function and seen in the wide boulevards and major building complexes, and a smaller, domestic, pedestrian-oriented scale within the neighborhood sectors. The most pronounced design failure of the city lies in the development of these residential districts, where a loose and monotonous pattern of building placement, excessive, unmaintained open space, and overscaled streets accord poorly with the prevailing lack of motors, and a climate characterized by dust storms, searing hot winds, and scorching sun. Although the standardized bazaar streets provided premises for relatively prosperous shop owners, no facilities were included in the scheme for the small peddlers and artisans so much a part of Indian town life.

Chandigarh embodied an attempt to apply Western conceptions of urban design to the Indian environment, with the result that the city lacks not only the spatial variety and visual interest, but the functional viability of a traditional Indian town. Indian vernacular building, employing narrow streets and a relatively dense pattern of inward-oriented courtyard houses, represents a far more sophisticated method of coming to terms with a tropical climate, a predominantly pedestrian environment, and a need for privacy than is evidenced in the misplaced Garden City ambient of Chandigarh.[114]

By and large, the development of the Punjab capital reveals an unimaginative application of urban design formula, rather than a sensitive awareness of the lively qualities of town life and the aesthetics of a nonmotorized urban environment. It may be noted, however, that the looseness of scale encountered in Chandigarh characterized much postwar design, and in Britain, where the climate and degree of mechanization would justify a more open urban pattern than in India, the first new towns were frequently criticized for their lack of compactness and urbanity.

In view of Le Corbusier's long concern with urban design it may seem strange that, having at last been given the opportunity to realize a city plan, he would largely abdicate responsibility for its development. Just as his earliest schematic designs had placed emphasis on the large-scale generalized aspects of the city, making little attempt at developing the more intimate texture, so in Chandigarh Le Corbusier restricted his planning efforts to delineating the major outlines of the master plan, and the creation of monumental complexes. He may have found the programmatic and technical restrictions of the project too hampering to justify a total involvement on his part. He had been unwilling to abandon Paris for an uninterrupted residence in India, and may have felt that his associates, residing on the site, would be better qualified to establish the residential pattern. He may also have sensed that his talents and predilections were primarily those of a monumental architect, and thus chose to dedicate himself to the sphere in which he excelled.

Just how the small-scale fabric of Chandigarh might have evolved at Le Corbusier's hand is uncertain. It could be argued that his fondness for Baroque expansiveness combined with his long-term obsession with the industrialized city had rendered him unsympathetic to the functional workings and aesthetic subtlety of the traditional Indian environment. Yet there is evidence that Le Corbusier was not insensitive to the indigenous building practices of hot, dry climates. In his North African travels he had admired and sketched Arab towns and houses, observing the dense ground coverage, the narrow streets, the buildings with blank external walls and sheltered internal courtyards. "While the street is a channel of violent movement," he noted, "your houses know nothing of it: they have closed the walls which face the street. It is within the walls that life blooms." Although his schematic designs consistently advocated an open urban pattern, in Algiers he praised the "pure and efficient stratification of the Casbah," pointing out that "among these terraces which form the roof of the city, not an inch is wasted."[115]

It is difficult, therefore, to predict with certainty what Le Corbusier might have produced in Chandigarh, had he elected to study local conditions and develop detailed sector layout and housing design. As the city now exists, it owes to him only its skeletal outlines, while the flesh and substance have been created by others. Nevertheless, Chandigarh remains the only realized scheme which can be directly attributed to Le Corbusier.

Toward the end of his life Le Corbusier added to the accumulation of unsuccessful competition designs which had characterized his work; his last project was a scheme submitted in 1958 for replanning the center of Berlin which had been destroyed in the Second World War (*Fig. 100*). In this project, he claimed to have been "faced with the problems which he had already studied for the center of Paris forty years earlier.... The time had come to take advantage of forty years of study and experimentation in architecture and planning."

The resulting scheme, which Le Corbusier termed an "excellent design conforming with the principles advocated by CIAM for thirty years,"[116] included adaptations of the architect's customary building types and patterns of building placement incorporated with a system of separated motor and pedestrian circulation. Although the jury included members presumed favorable to Le Corbusier, his plan was rejected.

NOTHING SUCCEEDS LIKE FAILURE

Recalling the time when he and his cousin were preparing the presentation for the City for Three Million, Le Corbusier recorded that, "During the exhausting hours of toil, in the middle of the night when we were bent over our drawings and despaired of ever completing them, I said to Pierre Jeanneret: 'We've got to do these drawings carefully, old man, we've got to go all the way. Just say to yourself that ten years or twenty years from now, they will still be called upon as witnesses; better still, that is when they will be published.'"[117] Le Corbusier appears to have underestimated the longevity of his scheme. The drawings were published sooner than he anticipated, and almost fifty years following their creation, their impact is still discernable.

Le Corbusier's place in the history of urban design must obviously derive from considerations other than direct planning practice, for if his reputation were to be based on realized plans, his position would be minor indeed. Le Corbusier's influence, although indirect, remains unquestioned. However, a sizeable body of modern civic design shows that after a lifetime of exhortation, his message, albeit in a garbled form, finally got through. Although his personal career had been studded with bitterness and failure, Le Corbusier succeeded in permeating the collective subconscious of the design profession with a set of urban prototypes forming a basis for much postwar building.

The magnitude of Le Corbusier's influence on urban design may be estimated somewhat by the opprobrium often attached to him, for although his own designs were consistently rejected by officialdom, he is sometimes held responsible for everything which is monotonous, mechanical, and overscaled in the modern environment. His seminal schemes, in the eyes of some, glamourized many of the worst features of modern cities, epitomizing and promoting a state of mind obsessed with form and oblivious to the humane aspects of the urban ambient.

Lewis Mumford, a lifelong decentrist, felt his opposition to Le Corbusier at an early date, recalling that, "from the time I read the first edition of his *Vers une architecture*, I knew that we were, by reason of our different temperaments and education, predestined enemies: he with his Cartesian clarity and his Cartesian elegance but also—alas!—with his Baroque insensitiveness to time, change, organic adaptation, functional fitness, ecological complexity; and, not least, with his sociological naiveté, his economic ignorance, and his political indifference. These very deficiencies were, as it turned out, what made his City of the Future such a successful model for world-wide imitation: its form reflected perfectly the financial, bureaucratic, and technological limitations of the present age."[118]

Declaring the imagery of the City for Three Million—which he termed "Yesterday's City of Tomorrow"—to have been the dominant influence in architecture and planning schools for thirty years, Mumford maintained, "The chief reason for Le Corbusier's immediate impact lies in the fact that he brought together the two architectural conceptions that separately have dominated the modern movement in architecture and city planning: the machine-made environment, standardized, bureaucratized, 'processed,' technically perfected to the last degree; and to offset this the natural environment, treated as so much visual open space, providing sunlight, pure air, green foliage, and views." Deeming the result of this fusion a "sterile hybrid," Mumford concluded pessimistically that "perhaps the very sterility of Le Corbusier's conception was what has made it so attractive to our age."[119]

Although it may be convenient to lay accusations regarding the inhumanity of scale and sterility of much modern planning at Le Corbusier's doorstep, one may reasonably consider his plans as insightful prophecy as well as inspiration. The pervasiveness of his imagery may be accounted for, not only by the immediate appeal of its romantic visualizations, but because Le Corbusier did in fact anticipate and synthesize in his designs future directions in urban development. His Voisin Plan for Paris, although unrealized, was prophetic of the massive urban renewal projects which would eventually transform the cores of many other cities. Le Corbusier did not invent the motor freeway, but he was one of the first to see it as the integral part of urban design which it has now become. He did not create the skyscraper, but foresaw its increasing dominance in the urban scene, and was highly sensitive to its aesthetic possibilities. Although Le Corbusier had been an early participant in the International Style in architecture, he can hardly, with justice, be held responsible for the slick and vapid conformity which characterized much postwar construction. His own work in architecture had evolved in a totally different direction, and he may more appropriately be blamed for having inspired some of the heavy-handed plasticity of overindividualized efforts. Although the skyscraper in a park, and indirectly, the skyscraper in a parking lot, may have been encouraged through his efforts, a general loosening of the urban fabric may be seen as the inevitable accompaniment of a growing dependence of the city on motor transport.

The postwar world has been characterized by a coarsening of urban texture, and the many design failures in accommodating juxtapositions of scale have underlined the weaknesses of Le Corbusier's prototypical schemes. Yet to claim that the poetic vision of the City for Three Million prepared the ground and set the standards for the frigid vacuity of the Paris and Milan suburbs, the stupefying scale of Soviet building, and the soulless high-rise barracks of American public housing is to credit Le Corbusier with an urban conception shared by no one else. In his advocacy of an urban pattern of widely separated, high-rise building and rigidly zoned activities, he was reinforcing the opinions of many modern designers who shared his reaction against the nineteenth-century heritage of urban congestion.[120] Le Corbusier's uniqueness lay in the comprehensiveness of his schemes, in the imagination and verve of his presentations, and the persistence with which he promoted his ideas.

In terms of postwar building, perhaps the most thoroughgoing adaptation of Le Corbusier's urban design conceptions may be seen in the capital of Brazil, begun in 1956 (*Figs. 101–102*). This new city, Brasilia, comprises a cross-axial plan, in which a sweeping motor freeway punctuates its intersection with a classically ordered government axis by means of a multilevel transport center. Bordering the freeway are residential superblocks containing standardized apartment blocks set amid open space, while the business center near the transportation hub is designed for unified high-rise building (*Fig. 102*). Although to some the new city seems to synthesize most of the weaknesses of a formalist approach to city planning, employing a static urban design of relentless monotony, to the Brazilian designers of the city, the image of technical mastery inherent in the freeways, the uniform modernity of the architecture, and the classical *partie* of the government complex, may embody an appropriate imagery for the new city. Built as part of an attempt to settle the Brazilian interior, Brasilia is indeed the "grip of man on nature," and for an undeveloped country the mechanistic formalism of the scheme may effectively symbolize a triumph of human will and organization over the hostile and sometimes overwhelming powers of nature.

In terms of the multifaceted activities of contemporary city planning, Le Corbusier's preoccupation with physical design may seem a willful disregard of other, possibly more crucial, aspects of the city. Present trends focus attention increasingly on the social aspects of the city, on the complex interaction of frequently explosive human forces. As mounting problems of the urban populace encourage a view of the city as primarily a sick social organism desperately in need of therapy, Le Corbusier's concern for the grand design may seem both irrelevant and anachronistic.

If current interest in city planning tends to emphasize social, rather than physical planning, within the realm of physical design, there is a growing reaction against many of Le Corbusier's design tenents, a distaste prompted by the large number of building projects which in a deplorable way seem to have employed many of his principles, frequently combining architectural regimentation with excessive open space to produce an environment hygienically ordered, but lifeless. The result has been a new appreciation of the aesthetics of urban "disorder," prompting some enthusiasts to examine and analyze formal configurations of hot dog stands, billboards, and used-car lots with the same reverence once devoted to classical ruins. As Camillo Sitte sought to derive ordering concepts from the irregularities of old European towns, so principles of urban vitality are now sought within the contemporary laissez-faire, Pop Art ambient. Replacing the ideal of overall control in urban design is a new advocacy of variety, spontaneity, and flexibility, coupled with a partial return to the Futurist conception of rapid obsolescence in the physical environment. In addition, the concept of rigid functional zoning has been replaced by a tendency to regard physical juxtaposition of housing, commerce, and institutions as essential to liveliness and convenience within the city.[121]

Although Le Corbusier's exhibition schemes were initially viewed by many as cities of the future, compared with some present-day projections for future cities, they appear remarkably old-fashioned, technically backward, and timid in scale. In an era which contemplates the housing of gigantic urban populations in towering megastructures or in underwater colonies, Le Corbusier's City for Three Million ceases to astound. Although Le Corbusier regarded himself, in comparison with Garden City enthusiasts, as an advocate of the large central city, he never envisioned populations of the size presently projected for many urban centers. Far from being terrifying images of the future, his visionary projects now begin to seem like a nostalgic view of the last moment when a city could be conceived in terms of a traditional, relatively permanent order, and manageable proportions.

Le Corbusier's most influential work epitomizes that optimistic peak of the modern movement marked by confidence in the splendors of a dawning new age, and a faith in advanced technology as a prime contributor to the solution of human problems. As the honeymoon of man and machine persisted, it remained possible to derive a romantic excitement from automobiles, airplanes, and tall buildings. Essentially, Le Corbusier sought to develop an urban scheme appropriate to what he grasped as the scale of modern technology, incorporating modern architecture with the ordering principles of the classical heritage and the picturesque attractions of nature. He sought to deal with essentials, presenting his ideas in a stripped-down generalized form. Le Corbusier was an artist looking at the city, and his schemes portrayed not cities, but ideas about cities. Allowing himself a certain poetic license, he outlined possibilities, simplifying the complexity of urban function for dramatic effect, and frequently leaving unfilled the gap between image and reality.

An accusation frequently made regarding much planning effort, including that of Le Corbusier, is that it is not sufficiently comprehensive, that it does not solve all urban, or indeed all human problems. This accusation, by and large, comes not from the public, but reflects the self-aggrandizing hubris of a planning profession which has come to regard itself as the sole custodian of human welfare. The fate of humanity, fortunately, does not lie in the keeping of any professional body, and should the human race ever achieve a perfection of happiness, wisdom, justice and spiritual enlightenment, it is not likely to be the result of good city planning.

Le Corbusier was an architect, and pretended to be nothing else. He did not attempt to master the technical aspects of city planning, and although he was confident that his civic designs would contribute to human well-being, he claimed to solve no social problems other than those responsive to changes in the physical environment.[122] He did not aim to reform or revolutionize society, but to provide an orderly physical framework within which the complex human drama might unfold. As a relatively consistent classicist, Le Corbusier regarded the formality of his schemes as in no way restrictive or inimical to a varied and vital urban life, but rather as a reflection of a human need for comprehensible, rational surroundings. If Le Corbusier's plans became a widely adopted model for modern urban design, a factor in rendering them acceptable may have been their embodiment of one of the oldest and most persistent traditions of visual order. In spite of a current fashion for spatial complexity which has led some designers to emulate the convolutions of Italian hill towns, Le Corbusier's prototypical solutions still provide simple, and in many instances, logical, points of reference.

In evaluating the long-range influence of Le Corbusier on city planning it is necessary to take into consideration not only the physical designs which he produced, but the impact of his voluminous writings and lectures. Perhaps no other architect of the modern movement so consistently exemplified its motivating spirit. Above all, the movement embodied a mood of hope, a genuine belief in progress and in a new efflorescence of human vitality. Le Corbusier, in turning his attentions to the city, denied the fear that the urban environment was an uncontrollable force, amorphous and chaotic. He affirmed the city as a man-made creation, the primary mark of mankind on earth, ordered by and subject to the human will. Tirelessly, relentlessly, through a lifetime of personal frustration, he promulgated the concept that human beings had power to control their destiny and mold their surroundings to human purpose. Conscious of the enormous organizational strength and the latent collective will of modern society, he sought to infuse others with his largeness of vision, indicating in his work a scale of action deemed necessary to achievement in the modern age. His designs were more than formal diagrams indicating patterns of building placement, they were exemplars of a scale of decision, a magnitude of effort. He never lost hope for the future, or wavered in the confidence that his efforts served mankind.

"And in the last resort, what does it matter to me whether people were happy or unhappy before the machine came? One thing I am certain of: the vast and agonized labor of the 19th century and the dramatic explosions that have begun the 20th are the heralds of a new age of harmony and joy. Just as the premonitory gleams of dawn in the east, as night dies, leave no doubt about the imminent appearance of the sun, so a thousand signs and concrete events are now affirming the imminent birth of a new era.

. . .

"The only possible road is that of enthusiasm. Postulating the existence of a modern consciousness and awakening that consciousness in all mankind. Solidarity, courage and order. A modern ethic. Already we are hurtling forward into the modern adventure. You think the time is not yet ripe? What terrible sounds, what rendings, what avalanches must assail your ears then, before they will hear? The thunder now rolling around the world fills the heart of the coward with fear and the hearts of the brave with joy.

. . .

"We meanwhile, stubbornly and tenderly, will continue to *make Plans*."[123]

NOTES

A CONTEMPORARY CITY

1. Le Corbusier, *Creation is a Patient Search* (New York: Frederick A. Praeger, 1966), p. 63.

2. Le Corbusier, *The City of To-morrow* (London: The Architectural Press, 1947), p. 163; first published in France as *Urbanisme* (Paris: Éditions Crès et Cie, 1925).

3. *Ibid.*, p. 164

4. *Ibid.*, p. xxi.

5. The reference is contained in Henry Lenning, *The Art Nouveau* (The Hague: Martinus Nijhoff, 1951), p. 24. (The wording is apparently a paraphrase).

6. Garnier's plan was not published until 1917, and its greatest influence dates from this time. The reader is referred to the companion volume in this series, *Tony Garnier: The Cité Industrielle* by Dora Wiebenson (New York: George Braziller, 1969).

7. Le Corbusier, *Towards a New Architecture* (New York: Frederick A. Praeger, 1959), p. 52. This book, first published in 1923 as *Vers une architecture* (Paris: Éditions Crès et Cie), constituted Le Corbusier's first major theoretical work.

8. *Ibid.*, p. 51.

9. Boccioni in his preface to the catalog of the first exhibition of Futurist painting in 1912. Quoted in Reyner Banham, *Theory and Design in the First Machine Age* (London: The Architectural Press, 1960), p. 102.

10. Antonio Sant'Elia in the introduction to his 1914 exhibition of the Città Nuova. Reproduced in Banham, *ibid.*, p. 129.

11. Le Corbusier, *The City of To-morrow*, p. 170.

12. *Ibid.*, p. xxv.

13. *Ibid.*, p. xxi.

14. *Ibid.*, p. 59.

15. *Ibid.*, p. 60.

16. *Ibid.*, p. 45.

17. The French edition of *Der Städtebau* with which Le Corbusier was familiar contained, in addition to other alterations of the original, a new chapter written by the translator Camille Martin, dealing with curving streets, and it is this addition which apparently formed the basis for much of Le Corbusier's criticism. For a clarification of Sitte's work see *Camillo Sitte and the Birth of Modern City Planning* by George R. and Christiane C. Collins (New York: Random House, 1965). Further discussion of the relation between Sitte and Le Corbusier may be found in S. D. Adshead, "Sitte and Le Corbusier," *Town Planning Review*, XIV (1930), 85–94, Percival and Paul Goodman, *Communitas, Means of Livelihood and Ways of Life* (Chicago: University of Chicago Press, 1947, passim), and Rudolph Wittkower, "Camillo Sitte's *Art of Building Cities* in an American Translation," *Town Planning Review*, XIX (1946–47), 164–169.

18. Le Corbusier, *The City of To-morrow*, p. xxv.

19. *Ibid.*, p. 8.

20. *Ibid.*, p. 17.

21. *Ibid.*, p. 37.

22. *Ibid.*, p. 10.

23. *Ibid.*, p. xxi.

24. *Ibid.*, p. 93.

25. *Ibid.*, p. 302.

26. *Ibid.*, p. 93.

27. *Ibid.*

28. Le Corbusier's usage of the term "Garden City" duplicates that employed by Georges Benoit-Lévy, a French advocate of the Garden City movement, and may have derived from him.

29. Le Corbusier, *The City of To-morrow*, p. 100. In spite of the fact that over two-thirds of the population of the City for Three Million would be residing in the "Garden Cities," these communities received relatively little attention in the overall design. Although the possibility of single-family houses is mentioned, the only housing which Le Corbusier developed for these areas was a type of apartment block similar to that employed in the central city, surrounded by sport grounds and communal garden allotments. Le Corbusier liked to refer to his apartment houses set amid open space as "vertical garden cities."

30. *Ibid.*, p. 72. The Abbé Laugier was an eighteenth-century French Jesuit priest and man of letters who published a work of architectural theory titled *Essai sur l'architecture* in 1753. Laugier encouraged a taste for simplicity, formal purity and structural sincerity, and is regarded as influential in the development of French neoclassicism.

31. *Ibid.*, p. 74.

32. *Ibid.*, p. 101. There is some ambiguity in Le Corbusier's discussion of population in the City of Three Million. He once described the distribution by stating, "in the centre, but only for purposes of daily toil, there would be 500,000 to 800,000 people; each evening the centre would be empty. The residential quarters of the city would absorb part, the garden cities the rest. Let us postulate then half a million citizens (around the centre) and two and a half millions in the garden cities" (*Ibid.*, p. 100). He also supplied a somewhat contradictory distribution of population by stating, "we have twenty-four skyscrapers capable each of housing 10,000 to 50,000 employees; this is the business and hotel section, etc., and accounts for 400,000 to 600,000 inhabitants. The residential blocks of the two main types already mentioned, account for a further 600,000 inhabitants. The garden cities give us a further 2,000,000 inhabitants, or more" (*Ibid.*, p. 172). It is this reference to the "400,000 to 600,000 inhabitants" in the city center which led to the assumption that Le Corbusier advocated skyscraper housing. How he intended to house these "inhabitants" is unclear, as the city center in the plan does not indicate any residential building.

33. Le Corbusier coined the word "Citrohan" as a pun on the "Citroën" automobile. "That is to say, a house like a motor-car, conceived and carried out like an omnibus or a ship's cabin. The actual needs of the dwelling can be formulated and demand their solution.... We must look upon the house as a machine for living in or as a tool" (*Towards a New Architecture*, p. 222). The first version of the Citrohan house was developed in 1920, the inspiration for its form having come from the design of a small truck drivers' restaurant in Paris. As described by Le Corbusier, "there was a bar (of zinc), kitchen in the back, a gallery which divided the height of the room; the front opened toward the street. One fine day we discovered this place and noticed that here all the elements were present that were necessary for the organization of a dwelling house.
"Simplification of light sources: only one large window at each end; two transverse bearing walls, a flat roof above—a box which could really be used as a house"— author's translation (*Œuvre complète 1910–29* [New York: George Wittenborn, 1964], p. 31; first published Zurich: Girsberger, 1929). This boxlike unit, adapted to apartment housing in the City for Three Million scheme, was later exhibited in the form of a full-scale model constructed for the Esprit Nouveau pavilion at the 1925 Paris Exposition of Decorative Art.

34. Author's translation—Le Corbusier, *Œuvre complète 1910–29*, p. 41.

35. Le Corbusier, *City of To-morrow*, p. 231. It may be noted that, although Le Corbusier advocated the employment of available technology in simplifying and mechanizing the household, his designs involved no technical innovations. Le Corbusier's rather orthodox conceptions of the dwelling may be contrasted with the experimental house produced by Buckminster Fuller in 1927. This dwelling unit, for which the word "Dymaxion" was coined in 1929, embodied a circular ring of dwelling space enclosed in a skin of plastic and hung by wires from an aluminum mast. The house was designed to be independent of the site, and could be broken down into packages for easy assembly and disassembly. Equipment designed by Fuller and projected for the house included automatic laundry and dishwashing machines, garbage disposal units, built-in vacuum cleaning, and anticipations of television, while the plumbing was redesigned to require no sewer and water connections. Apartment housing was conceived as a series of deck planes suspended by tension cables from a central tower of inflated duraluminum tubes, and containing a central service core.

36. *Ibid.*, pp. 188–189.

37. *Ibid.*, p. 177.

38. *Ibid.*, p. 236.

39. *Ibid.*, p. 178.

40. *Ibid.*

41. *Ibid.*, p. 193.

42. *Ibid.*, p. 57.

43. Lewis Mumford, "Yesterday's City of To-morrow," *Architectural Record*, CXXXII (November, 1962), 141. It may be noted that Le Corbusier himself had doubts regarding the scale of open space when he was first developing his scheme, reporting, "I was filled with a great anguish lest the immense open spaces that I was creating in our imaginary city, spaces dominated by the wide sky on all sides, should be 'dead' spaces; I was afraid that they would prove full only of boredom, and that the inhabitants of such a city would be seized by panic at the sight of so much emptiness" (*The Radiant City* [New York: The Orion Press, 1967], p. 106; first published in France as *La ville radieuse* [Boulogne (Seine): Éditions de l'Architecture d'Aujourd'hui 1935]). The feeling of panic to which Le Corbusier alluded had been noted by nineteenth-century physicians who used the term "agoraphobia" (literally "fear of the agora") to describe the uneasiness which seized many people when subjected to excessive urban space. Sitte used the term *Platzscheu* to describe the same affliction.

44. Le Corbusier, *The City of To-morrow*, pp. 239–240.

45. This criticism, which appeared in *L'Architecte* in 1925, was quoted by Le Corbusier in *The City of To-morrow*, p. 133. Needless to say, Le Corbusier did not agree with such commentary, contemptuously ridiculing the doctrine of "people who are terrified by any simple statement of fact; that doctrine is 'Life'; life with its many facets and unending variety; life, two-faced or four-faced, putrescent or healthy, limpid or muddy; the exact and the arbitrary, logic and illogicality, the Good God and the good Devil; everything in confusion; you pour it all in, stir well and serve hot and label the pot 'Life'" (*Ibid.*, p. 17).

46. *Ibid.*, pp. 277–278.

47. *Ibid.*, p. 287.

48. *Ibid.*

49. *Ibid.*, pp. 282–283.

50. *Ibid.*, p. 296.

51. *Ibid.*, p. 288.

THE RADIANT CITY

52. Le Corbusier, *The Radiant City*, p. 43.

53. *Ibid.*, p. 143. An interest in creating analogies between organisms and cities may be seen in Le Corbusier's first book on civic design, *The City of To-morrow*. In the French edition(*Urbanisme*), an appendix was included in which biological drawings were presented as models of systematic functioning. A diagram of the heart and intestinal system was accompanied by the caption, "Transport. Motor center. Grand traverses. Sorting house. Services."

54. Le Corbusier, *Creation is a Patient Search*, p. 155.

55. The neighborhood-unit concept involved an attempt to plan housing in terms of a population unit, with provision for community services included in the residential area. The earliest realization of the neighborhood unit in modern planning is believed to be Forest Hills Gardens, a model neighborhood developed by Clarence Perry for the Russell Sage Foundation, and built on Long Island between 1911 and 1913. Perry subsequently published his conceptions of neighborhood and community planning as part of the *Regional Survey of New York and its Environs in 1929*. He felt that the basic residential unit should contain the population which could be served by one elementary school (approximately 6,000 people) and that, in addition to housing, the neighborhood should provide parks and recreation areas, local shops and civic institutions, and an internal street system designed for specific local use. Surrounding the neighborhood would be arterial streets. Variations of the neighborhood-unit idea occurred in Sunnyside Gardens in New York, designed by Clarence Stein and Henry Wright in 1924, and in Radburn, New Jersey, in 1929. The Radiant City neighborhood unit of 2,700 people was based on the projected size of an apartment house rather than on any functional analysis of community needs or characteristics.

56. Le Corbusier, *The Radiant City*, p. 171. As evidence of the military value of his scheme, Le Corbusier cited a book published in 1930 by Lieutenant Colonel Vauthier, Inspector General of Aerial Defense for the national territory, titled *Danger from the Air and This Country's Future*. With regard to the redevelopment of Paris, Vauthier had concluded, "Our preferences, in the matter of large cities, must go in every case to the Le Corbusier system."

114

57. *Ibid.*, p. 321.

58. *Ibid.*, p. 197.

59. *Ibid.*, p. 321.

60. *Ibid.*, p. 326.

61. *Ibid.*, p. 321. A recognition of the highway as the basis for a rural reorganization may also be found in Frank Lloyd Wright's decentrist Broadacre City scheme of the 1930's.

62. *Ibid.*, p. 327.

63. *Ibid.*, p. 197.

VARIATIONS ON A THEME

64. Le Corbusier, *The City of To-morrow*, p. 301.

65. Quoted in J. Tyrwhitt, J. L. Sert, E. N. Rogers, *The Heart of the City* (London: Lund Humphries, 1952), p. 171.

66. Le Corbusier, *Œuvre complète 1934–38* (New York: George Wittenborn, 1964), p. 28; first published Zurich: Girsberger, 1939. Le Corbusier was particularly enthusiastic about the development of the residential district in Nemours, and he unsuccessfully sought to organize land acquisition of the area before it could fall prey to speculators or be parceled out in a manner destructive to overall planning.

67. Le Corbusier, *The Radiant City*, p. 177.

68. *Ibid.*, p. 207.

69. Le Corbusier, *The City of To-morrow*, p. 301. For other criticisms of the social philosophy of Le Corbusier's cities, see Appendix.

70. *Ibid.*

71. Le Corbusier, *The Radiant City*, p. 9.

72. From a report by S. Gorny written in October, 1930, on the subject of Le Corbusier's proposals for Moscow. Reproduced in *The Radiant City*, p. 46.

73. This description of Le Corbusier is recounted by Gordon Stephenson in "Le Corbusier," a paper read before the Vitruvian Society, Toronto. *Royal Architectural Institute of Canada Journal*, XXXIII (June, 1956), 201. It was Commissar Lunacharsky who promoted official opposition to modern architecture in the early 1930's, the turning point in policy centering on the international design competition for the Palace of the Soviets in 1931. During the 1920's the Soviet Union had sponsored notable efforts in experimental architecture, a circumstance which had prompted Le Corbusier and other modern architects to submit innovative schemes for the projected palace. The sharp reversal in government policy, however, removed all nontraditional schemes from consideration, and Soviet architecture henceforth adopted a style of conservative classicism. Le Corbusier's Ministry of Light Industry building in Moscow, begun in 1929 and completed in 1934, was an object of intensive criticism by Lunacharsky who employed it as evidence of the failings of modern design.

74. Le Corbusier, *The Four Routes* (London: Dennis Dobson Ltd., 1947), p. 126; first published as *Sur les 4 routes* (Paris: Gallimard, 1941).

75. At the time Le Corbusier visited Rio de Janeiro, another Frenchman, Alfred Agache, was engaged in developing a master plan for the city. Agache was an academic classicist, and Le Corbusier had been somewhat hesitant in appearing in Rio to present views which must inevitably conflict with those of his countryman.

Although he had initially agreed to speak only regarding his ideals of architecture and his plan for Paris, Le Corbusier could not resist the seduction of the Rio landscape, informing his audience, "I swore to myself not to open my mouth about Rio. And here I find myself with an irresistible need to speak"—author's translation (*Précisions sur un état présent de l'architecture et de l'urbanisme* [Paris: Éditions Crès et Cie, 1930; reprinted Éditions Vincent, Fréal et Cie, 1960], p. 236). Relations between Agache and Le Corbusier seem to have been not altogether unfriendly, and Agache is reported to have described Le Corbusier to the Prefect by stating, "Le Corbusier is a man who shatters windows, a man who makes the wind blow, and we others, we follow after him"—author's translation (*Ibid.*, p. 237). Although Le Corbusier seems to have refrained from overt criticism of the Agache plan for Rio during his visit, he later employed an illustration from this scheme in *The Radiant City* over the caption, "Here a city planner of the classical school has once again proposed courtyards and corridor-streets" (*The Radiant City*, p. 223).

In 1936 Le Corbusier revisited Rio at the request of the Minister of Education to advise on the design of a new Ministry of Education building. At this time he also projected a new plan for the University of Rio.

76. Le Corbusier, *The Home of Man* (New York: Frederick A. Praeger, 1948), p, 135; first published in France as *La Maison des hommes* (Paris: Librarie Plon, 1941).

77. Le Corbusier, *Œuvre complète 1946–52* (New York: George Wittenborn, 1964), p. 76; first published Zurich: Girsberger, 1953.

78. Authors translation—Le Corbusier, *Précisions*, pp. 234–236.

79. *Ibid.*, p. 244.

80. *Ibid.*, p. 245. A later project derived from Le Corbusier's scheme may be seen in Geoffrey Jellicoe, *Motopia* (New York: Frederick A. Praeger, 1961), a visionary proposal in which a continuous apartment block carrying a rooftop motor road is extended throughout the landscape in the form of a giant grid.

    Le Corbusier produced a modified version of his Rio scheme in 1936 in which the entire ground area was shown free of building except for widely spaced skyscrapers and the linear apartment freeway.

81. Le Corbusier's plans for Algiers were initiated in 1931, when he was invited by a citizens group called The Friends of Algiers to lecture on "the architectural revolution achieved by modern techniques" and "how the architectural revolution can solve the problem of urbanization in big cities." (*The Radiant City*, p. 228). In citing the need for comprehensive city planning in Algiers, Le Corbusier described the city as no longer a provincial colonial center, but the head of the African continent, and part of a new economic grouping centering on the Mediterranean and including Paris, Barcelona, Rome, and Algiers.

82. *Ibid.*, p. 247.

83. *Ibid.*, p. 260.

84. Le Corbusier, *When the Cathedrals Were White* (New York: Reynal & Hitchcock, 1947), p. 90.

85. *Ibid.*, p. 51.

86. *Ibid.*, p. 56.

87. *Ibid.*, pp. 41–42.

88. *Ibid.*, p. 153.

89. *Ibid.*, p. 86.

90. *Ibid.*, p. 87.

91. Le Corbusier, *The Home of Man*, p. 70.

92. The idea of the linear city in which a pattern of building parallels a line of transportation, was first promulgated in 1882 by a Spaniard, Arturo Soria y Mata, who projected and partially built a linear project in which building plots extended along a tramline surrounding Madrid. Seeing the linear urban form as embodying limitless possibilities for extension, Soria y Mata once speculated that such a city could extend from "Cadiz to St. Petersburg, from Peking to Brussels." Detailed consideration of the work of Soria y Mata may be found in George R. Collins, "The Ciudad Lineal of Madrid," *Journal of the Society of Architectural Historians*, XVIII (May, 1959), 38–54, and *Arturo Soria y la Ciudad Lineal* (Madrid, 1968). Additional consideration of linear city planning by George R. Collins may be found in "Linear Planning Throughout the World," *Journal of the Society of Architectural Historians*, XVIII (October, 1959), 74–93; *Pedestrian in the City (Architects' Year Book, XI)*; and "Linear Planning, Its Forms and Functions," Dutch *Forum*, XX, No. 5 (March, 1968), 2–26.

    The sources of Le Corbusier's ideas of linear planning are uncertain. He was familiar with Soviet theorists, and may also have been influenced by the French economist, Charles Gide, who was an advocate of linear planning.

93. Le Corbusier, *Concerning Town Planning* (New Haven: Yale University Press, 1948), p. 46; first published in France as *Propos d'urbanisme* (Paris: Éditions Bourrelier, 1946).

94. *Ibid.*, p. 122.

95. Le Corbusier, *The Home of Man*, p. 73.

96. Le Corbusier, *L'Urbanisme des trois établissements humains* (Paris: Éditions de Minuit, 1959), p. 129; first published in 1944.

97. Le Corbusier, *Œuvre complète 1952–57* (New York: George Wittenborn, 1964), p. 176; first published Zurich: Girsberger, 1957.

98. Fourier first expounded his theories in 1808, and continued presentation of his ideas through publishing a series of newspapers, *Le Phalanstère ou la Réforme Industrielle* (1832–34), *La Phalange* (1836–43), and *La Démocratie Pacifique* (1843–50). He conceived of his community as a way to achieve universal harmony through a balance

of human character types. Fourier had considerable impact in the United States, where his admirers included Horace Greeley, editor of the *New York Tribune*, and his concepts influenced the organization of the Brook Farm community. Fourier's ideas were put into partial effect by Charles Godin, an industrialist who in 1859 adapted the *phalanstère* idea to a scheme for housing the workers of his iron foundry at Guise; the communal dwelling was called a *familistère*. Le Corbusier was familiar with Fourier, and made reference to him in *The Marseilles Block* (London: Harvill Press, 1953). For further discussion of Le Corbusier's conception of community see Peter Serenyi, "Le Corbusier, Fourier and the Monastery at Ema," *Art Bulletin*, XLIX (December, 1967), 277–286.

99. Lewis Mumford, "The Sky Line: The Marseilles 'Folly,'" *The New Yorker*, XXXIII (October 5, 1957), 92. Visiting the building five years after its opening Mumford observed that the chief surviving shop within the Unité was a small general store. The laundry had not been able to operate successfully, and the restaurant and hotel were lacking. In the second Unité, at Nantes, Le Corbusier attempted to provide the shops with more patronage by placing them at ground level.

CHANDIGARH

100. A Polish architect, Matthew Nowicki, who had been associated with Mayer in the creation of the initial plan for Chandigarh, was to have been retained by the Punjab government to supervise the architectural development of the city. His death in an airplane crash in 1950 necessitated that a new designer be engaged, and because of the difficulty of finding dollars, the search was limited to soft currency areas. The selection of the second group of designers was made by P. L. Varma, the Chief Engineer of Punjab, and P. N. Thapar, a government administrator.

Maxwell Fry, Jane Drew, and Pierre Jeanneret joined the project with three-year contracts as senior architects working in Chandigarh, while Le Corbusier was engaged as architectural advisor with the stipulation that he pay two annual visits of one month each to the site. Following the expiration of the three-year contract, Fry and Drew returned to England, while Pierre Jeanneret remained in Chandigarh, directing the Capital Project Office until 1965. Pierre Jeanneret eventually assumed the rank of Chief Architect and Planner of Punjab, and in this capacity adapted the Chandigarh plan to a linear configuration in the design of Talwara Township. In this scheme, a row of residential sectors, similar to the Chandigarh sectors, was projected parallel to a belt of industrial establishments, a railroad line and a motor highway. For a complete account of the planning of Chandigarh, see Norma Evenson, *Chandigarh* (Berkeley: University of California Press, 1966).

101. Quoted in L. R. Nair, *Why Chandigarh?* (Simla: Publicity Department, Punjab Government, 1950), p. 6. The province of Punjab, as reorganized after the Indian partition, contained a population of Hindi-speaking Hindus and Punjabi-speaking Sikhs. Within the Sikh population, a desire arose for a separate state, and in 1966, following years of chronic agitation and political pressure from the Sikhs, the central government divided the province, creating the present Sikh state of Punjab and the Hindu state of Haryana. Chandigarh was made a federal Union Territory serving as a joint capital for both states.

102. Le Corbusier, *Œuvre complète 1946–52*, p. 11.

103. Christopher Rand, "City on a Tilting Plain," *The New Yorker*, XXXI (April 30, 1955), 42.

104. Le Corbusier, paper delivered at a press conference at the Palais de la Découverte, March 18, 1953.

105. The golden section is a proportion devised by the ancient Greeks, embodying the division of a line or geometrical figure in such a way that the smaller dimension is to the greater as the greater to the whole. A golden rectangle is one in which the width is to the length as the length is to the sum of the two ($a : b = b : a + b$). Le Corbusier's system of proportioning, the Modulor, relates somewhat in concept to the systems of harmonic proportioning characteristic of Renaissance theorists, and to their belief in a correspondence between human proportions and those of architecture. Essentially, the Modulor is a series of proportions based on the measurements of a six-foot human figure in various attitudes such as sitting, standing, resting, etc. Two series of measurements were developed, one based on a standing human figure, and the other on a figure with an upraised arm. As described by Le Corbusier, "The Modulor is a measuring tool based on the human body and on mathematics. A man with arm upraised provides, at the determining points of his occupation of space—foot, solar plexis, head, tips of fingers of the upraised arm—three intervals which give rise to a

117

series of golden sections called the Fibonacci series" (*The Modulor*, p. 55, see below). The Modulor was to combine two modules in one—a module of measurement and a module of scale. In addition to providing a way of proportioning structures, the Modulor values would furnish a means of converting calculations from the metric system to foot and inch measurements. It was also hoped by Le Corbusier that the system would be useful in establishing universal proportions for the prefabrication of building components and for industrial products. Le Corbusier presented his conception of the Modulor in two books, *The Modulor* (Cambridge: Harvard University Press, 1954); first published Boulogne (Seine): Éditions de l'Architecture d'Aujourd' hui, 1950; and *Modulor 2* (Cambridge: Harvard University Press, 1958); first published Paris: Éditions de l'Architecture d'Aujourd'hui, 1955. For commentaries on the Modulor see Boyd (1957), Collins (1954), Ghyka (1948), and Wittkower, *Four Great Makers of Modern Architecture* (1963).

106. Le Corbusier had wished to have the V designation included in all street names, explaining that "when one says: 'Republic Boulevard' or 'Lotus Street' no notion has been evoked. But if you say: 'the V2 Republic' or 'Lotus V5,' everything becomes explicit; one knows instantly the nature of the ways (or streets), their importance, their location in town, etc." (Le Corbusier, "The Master Plan", *Marg*, XV, [December, 1961], 9). Le Corbusier's recommendations, however, were not followed in the naming of Chandigarh streets.

107. Quoted in Rand, *op. cit.*, p. 50. (see note 103).

108. Le Corbusier, *Modulor II*, p. 215.

109. Quoted in Le Corbusier, *Œuvre complète 1946–52*, p. 157.

110. Le Corbusier, "The Monuments," *Marg*, XV (December, 1961), insert between pp. 10–11.

111. Le Corbusier, *Modulor II*, p. 254.

112. Le Corbusier, *Œuvre complète 1946–52*, p. 159.

113. The statement was written by P. L. Varma, Chief Engineer of Punjab.

114. Generally speaking, during the period of British colonialism, little effort had been made to harmonize urban planning with local vernacular. An exception to this occurred in the work of Patrick Geddes who, between 1915 and 1919, made planning reports for eighteen Indian cities. Geddes consistently advocated conservative planning, retaining the virtues while attempting to remedy the defects of the existing environment. In general, Indian planning and architectural education continues to be dominated by foreign ideas, and the defects of Chandigarh, although initially attributable to foreign architects, might as easily have been produced by Indian designers. Chandigarh entered a second phase of planning following Le Corbusier's death, Jeanneret's retirement, and the political reorganization of the city as a federal Union Territory serving two provinces newly created from the division of Punjab. The Indian planners of the second phase have announced the intention of improving patterns of building placement, providing more plentifully for small commerce and seeking to develop a greater sense of community.

115. Le Corbusier, *The Radiant City*, p. 230.

116. Le Corbusier, *Œuvre complète 1957–65* (Zurich: Girsberger, 1965), p. 230.

NOTHING SUCCEEDS LIKE FAILURE

117. Le Corbusier, *The Radiant City*, p. 204.

118. Lewis Mumford, "Architecture as a Home for Man," *Architectural Record*, CXLIII (February, 1968), 114.

119. Lewis Mumford, "Yesterday's City of Tomorrow," *Architectural Record*, CXXXII (November, 1962), 141. For further reference to Le Corbusier's critics, see Appendix.

120. Walter Gropius, for example, advocated a form of urban housing similar to that suggested by Le Corbusier, recommending in a paper delivered to the 1930 C.I.A.M. Congresses a pattern of widely separated rows of ten-to-twelve-story apartment blocks. Like Le Corbusier, he sought to end the "corridor street" and achieve a looser urban fabric. Explaining his ideas, he stated, "The city needs to reassert itself. It needs the stimulus resulting from a development of housing peculiarly its own, a type which will combine a maximum of air, sunlight and open parkland with a minimum of distances and communications and minumum running costs. Such conditions can be fulfilled by the multi-story apartment block, and consequently its development should be one of the urgent tasks of city planning.... The family house, then is no panacea since its logical consequence would be a dispersal and denial of the city. The *loosening* but not the *breaking-up* of the city should be the aim. The two

opposites 'town' and 'country' can be brought closer to each other through our use of the technical resources which we have at our disposal, and through the most extensive landscaping of all the available ground, even the rooftops, so that the encounter with nature will become a daily and not merely a Sunday experience..." (Quoted in Sigfried Giedion, *Walter Gropius—Work and Teamwork* [New York: Reinhold Publishing Corp. 1954], pp. 80–81).

121. Criticism of the overordered environment has paralleled much postwar building. As the British New Towns began to take form, they were increasingly criticized for a lack of urbanity; Gorden Cullen observed that "One of the essential qualities of a town is that it is a gathering together of people and utilities for the generation of civic warmth. However overcrowded, dingy, insanitary and airless the old towns may be, most of them retain this quality, which is the essential quality without which a town is no town, *with which* lack of air is merely a minor nuisance—let us call it towniness" ("Prairie Planning in the New Towns," *Architectural Review*, CXIV [July, 1953], 34). See also J. M. Richards, "The Failure of the New Towns," *Architectural Review*, CXIV (July, 1953), 28–32. In her much-discussed book, *The Death and Life of Great American Cities* (New York: Random House, 1961), Jane Jacobs combined incisive criticism of current city planning practice, with an analysis of the complex functioning of the existing urban environment. Deploring the rigidity of much urban design, she maintained that "*A city cannot be a work of art....* To approach a city, or even a city neighborhood, as if it were a larger architectural problem, capable of being given order by converting it into a disciplined work of art, is to make the mistake of attempting to substitute art for life" (p. 373). In her discussions of the factors inherent in urban vitality, she condemned the hygienic but dangerous isolation of many redevelopment and housing projects, stressing a need for high building densities and abolition of the superblock in favor of small blocks and numerous streets. Instead of rigidly zoned districts, she advocated variety and spontaneity of growth through encouragement of mixed-use areas containing a diversity of housing, commerce, and institutional facilities.

Further support for the spontaneous nondesigned urban environment may be found in the writings of Robert Venturi, whose book *Complexity and Contradiction in Architecture* (New York: Museum of Modern Art, 1966) was introduced by Professor Vincent Scully of Yale as "probably the most important writing on the making of architecture since Le Corbusier's *Vers une architecture*, of 1923." Attacking the advocates of what he deemed a false simplicity in the urban order, Venturi observed, "The seemingly chaotic juxtapositions of honky-tonk elements express an intriguing kind of vitality and validity, and they produce an unexpected approach to unity as well.... Some of the vivid lessons of Pop Art, involving contradictions of scale and context, should have awakened architects from prim dreams of pure order, which, unfortunately, are imposed in the easy gestalt unities of the urban renewal projects of establishment Modern architecture.... And it is perhaps from the everyday landscape, vulgar and disdained, that we can draw the complex and contradictory order that is valid and vital for our architecture as an urbanistic whole" (pp. 102–103). To illustrate Venturi's belief that the designer must learn to understand the workings of the seemingly disordered unplanned environment, he published an analytical study of the Las Vegas strip, titled "A Significance for A&P Parking Lots or Learning from Las Vegas," (*Architectural Forum*, CXXVIII [March, 1968], 36–43). He began his study by stating, "Learning from the existing landscape is a way of being revolutionary for an architect. Not the obvious way, which is to tear down Paris and begin again, as Le Corbusier suggested in the 1920's, but another way which is more tolerant: that is to question how we look at things" (p. 36).

122. Le Corbusier felt that members of the design profession should not venture into fields other than their own, advising his colleagues at the 1930 C.I.A.M. Congress as follows: "Contemporary architecture and especially city planning are direct results of the social situation; this goes without saying. By means of personal inquiries let's keep up to date with the present evolution but, I beg of you, let's not get into politics or sociology here, in the midst of our Congress. They are too endlessly complex phenomena; economics are closely linked to them. We are not competent to discuss these intricate questions here. I repeat: here we should remain architects and city planners and on this professional basis we should make known to those whose duty they are, the possibilities afforded by modern techniques and the need for a new kind of architecture and city planning" (*The Radiant City*, p. 37).

123. *Ibid.*, pp. 342–343.

APPENDIX:

LE CORBUSIER'S CRITICS

Although it would be mistaken to assume that Le Corbusier's urban design received no praise, it is true that his work appears to have offered something for almost every type of critic. His visionary schemes attracted unfavorable mention from both decentrists and centrists, aesthetes and pragmatists, were condemned as both communist and capitalist, and attacked on visual, functional, and social grounds. Even those who admired his designs, sometimes complained that they were not comprehensive enough.

The simplification of building types and architectural uniformity in Le Corbusier's early urban schemes was viewed as the destruction of traditional aesthetic richness and variety; an English critic observed of the City for Three Million, "Not a dome or a spire is to be seen; nor, indeed, any other architectural feature of special interest. It appears just as if the forms of building had been subject to some severe and ultra-Puritan censorship, and only two or three, counted innocuous and pure had been allowed to survive.... It is much too easy to design ideal or Utopian cities if the artist concentrates upon two or three of the factors to be considered and rejects all the others. M. Le Corbusier's city is a dead city and it represents nothing more or less than architectural nihilism" (Trystan Edwards, "The Dead City," *Architectural Review*, LXVI [September, 1929], 135).

In addition to criticism directed at the architecture, the treatment of open space was often condemned as a negation of traditional concepts of urban enclosure. "Le Corbusier's plans seem to show a casual disregard for the urban concept of 'containment' of open space that people seem to expect and desire in cities. He lets his open areas flow all over the place" (H. A. Anthony, "Le Corbusier: His Ideas for Cities," *American Institute of Planners Journal*, XXXII [September, 1966], 287).

Although many saw Le Corbusier's schemes as a glorification of the large central city, his extensive employment of open area prompted Jane Jacobs, in her advocacy of high-density settlement, to relegate Le Corbusier to the sphere of Garden City designers. She maintained that, "ironically, the Radiant City comes directly out of the Garden City. Le Corbusier accepted the Garden City's fundamental image, superficially at least, and worked to make it practical for high densities.... Le Corbusier's Radiant City depended upon the Garden City. The Garden City planners and their ever-increasing following among housing reformers, students and architects were indefatigably popularizing the ideas of the super-block, the project neighborhood, the unchangeable plan, and grass, grass, grass; what is more they were successfully establishing such attributes as the hallmarks of humane, socially responsible, functional, high-minded planning. Le Corbusier really did not have to justify his vision in either humane or city-functional terms. If the great object of city planning was that Christopher Robin might go hoppety-hoppety on the grass, what was wrong with Le Corbusier?" (*The Death and Life of Great American Cities* [New York: Random House, 1961], p. 22).

In addition to objections to the urban aesthetics of Le Corbusier's plans, critics were not slow to point out their functional weaknesses. The failure of the City for Three Million to provide for expansion was noted, together with the functional inflexibility of its standardized building. The uniform high-rise office building was deemed inadequate for varied commercial uses, and the apartment housing unsuitable for many dwelling needs. Frederick Hiorns, in his survey, *Town Building in History* (London: Harrap, 1956), described Le Corbusier's high-rise housing as both impractical and unsafe, apprehensively citing "the dangers to occupants (many hundreds of people, perhaps) from fire or panic and failure of the means of escape," and condemning the overall civic design as an "evasion of the problem of a natural, safe, and convenient form of life" (p. 354).

The traffic system seemed both unrealistic in terms of parking facilities, and hazardous in its encouragement of high speeds. To critics of the 1920's, the width of the projected roadways seemed excessive for traffic needs, and in a later age, familiar with the urban freeway, it was observed, "Le Corbusier brought the fast moving automobile through the city, through its very heart, not around it, and thus he built in a powerful destructive force.... With our current experience of urban traffic volumes, we can see that the broad arteries of Le Corbusier's ideal cities would discourage human contact across them, and would separate people and divide the city into triangular and rectangular sections" (Anthony, "Le Corbusier...," p. 286).

Although Le Corbusier had not attempted to formulate a specific social philosophy, and had considered his work as primarily a technical contribution, many observers deplored the social implications of his schemes. In the view of Hiorns, Le Corbusier advocated that "what is now so fittingly developed might be substituted by a Wellsian-robot way of life. Neither verbal nor graphic dexterity can be a substitute for critical judgment and a correct appreciation of the inbred, fundamentally unchanging, cultural, social, and domestic preferences of mankind" (Hiorns, *Town Building*, p. 355). To some, the uniformity of the city epitomized the regimented anonymity of the modern superstate; S. D. Adshead observed of Le Corbusier that "He regards humanity (if such a word can be used to express a crowd of his men) as consisting of innumerable pawns to be driven into cubicles along straight channels. He is a communist who plans his city on the principles of cellular formation, and he forces his citizens into moulds" ("Camillo Sitte and Le Corbusier," *Town Planning Review*, XIV [November, 1930], 92).

The opinion expressed by some Russians in the 1930's that Le Corbusier's urban plans symbolized bourgeois commercialism was echoed by Percival and Paul Goodman in *Communitas, Means of Livelihood and Ways of Life*, (Chicago: University of Chicago Press, 1947). Viewing Le Corbusier's civic designs as a glorification of finance capitalism and a perpetuation of class distinction, they claimed, "the Ville Radieuse is the perfecting of a status quo, 1925, that as an ideal has perished already" (p. 28).

To a postwar generation searching for new social ideals, Le Corbusier seemed to stand reprehensibly aloof from social reform. It was observed that "Le Corbusier, so far as one can tell, still accepts this age with its restless getting and spending, its lethal, debt-ridden commercialism, its sub-human shuttlecock automatons, its schizophrenic outbursts. He never seriously questions its validity, being too engrossed in his specialized, architectural enthusiasms. He has never committed himself to any political creed, and he tells us frankly that he does not dedicate his work either to our existing bourgeois capitalist society or to the Third International—as though there were no alternative. 'It is a technical work,' he says with disarming naivety. Yet how can the planner, or indeed the architect, any longer avoid political questions and the philosophical and economic ideas which support them? Planning *is* politics, whether you like it or not.... For all his stimulus, Le Corbusier cannot buoy us up indefinitely with his vivid but purely architectural philosophy. A far wider hope is needed now, ...something far more energizing than the vision of a wider, cleaner workhouse quadrangle—even if a tree has been planted in the middle" (Eric de Maré, "What Kind of Tomorrow?" *Architectural Review*, CIII [June, 1948], 273.

Another critic opined that, "Le Corbusier spent his whole life concerning himself with his fellow man, but his concept of that man tended to be stereotyped and modeled on himself." Viewing Le Corbusier's sense of community as essentially authoritarian and monastic, he concluded that "the shortcomings of the Radiant City are not so much technical or quantitative; the main defects of the concept are on the fundamental, qualitative level of urban psychology" (Ervin Galantay, "Corbu's Tightrope," *Progressive Architecture*, XLVIII [June, 1967], 198–206).

Although the sweeping scale of change epitomized in Le Corbusier's schemes had alarmed some observers, he was also criticized for not going far enough. He seemed to have little concern for the implementation of planning, one critic commenting that "he waxes eloquent, confident and condescending over the physical aspects of city planning, tosses aside the only question on ways and means with an ambiguous: 'FINANCE? To see that the house is without walls and without a roof, its foundation shattered. To take off one's jacket, roll up one's sleeve and get started. Let the farmer farm, the bricklayer lay bricks, and the manufacturer manufacture. One eats to live; one does not live to eat. Translate into the language of finance.' ...In his writing the incessant repetition of such glorious simplifications is as useless as it is monotonous and, except for first rung disciples, pretty unconvincing. Le Corbusier, however, is but one of several superior minds of our day who can never seem to breach the gap between reality and Utopia to the satisfaction of the everyday man on whom they must depend for the dirty work..." (M. S., Review of *Concerning Town Planning, Architectural Forum*, LXXXVIII [June, 1948], 170–171).

William Holford felt that Le Corbusier's schemes, by their static nature, might fail to accord with the speed of social and economic changes in the modern world. "The objectives so brilliantly described by Le Corbusier will take time to be accepted by society as a whole, and still longer to be realized in terms of city reconstruction and new building. By that time the pattern of daily life may be as different from what it is today as post-war society is from pre-war. And it may be that some of the structural and spatial principles...

will continue to be valid, and that others will not. The finite town of tomorrow may be the dying town of the day after" ("Architecture Above All," *Architectural Review*, CIII [February, 1948], 68).

Although admiring the design of Le Corbusier's Radiant City when it was introduced, Erwin Gutkind felt that "he does not go far enough.... This theory itself is thirty years behind. The central problem of town planning is today no more 'town' planning—not any more the problem of the metropolis or the big town—but the planning of the whole of a country, at the least of large connected territories.... The realization of his proposals can never be a solution or a real new creation in the deepest sense but would only be, even in the best cases, a slum clearance in the most sublime form.... We must demand the replacement of 'La Ville Radieuse' by 'La Totalité Du Pay Radieux' " ("The Indivisible Problem," *Architectural Review*, LXXX [October, 1936], 172).

As the scope of city and regional planning became more technically complex, Le Corbusier, with his grandiose simplicities, came to stand increasingly isolated from the mainstream of the planning profession. Although, during the war years, Le Corbusier had expanded his considerations to project a schematic pattern of regional settlement embodying linear-industrial cities connecting radio-concentric centers, this scheme was unrelated to any economic base, and, like his earlier civic plans, appeared primarily an arbitrary physical ordering, rather than a response to the varied factors which promote urban growth. However he expanded his vision, Le Corbusier seemed unable to bridge the gap between design and planning.

From the beginning to the end of his career, Le Corbusier's critics would insist that, for all the outward appeal of many of his designs, he had avoided coming to grips with many of the real problems of the city, and an observation made by Trystan Edwards in 1929 was still being echoed thirty years later. "The real effect of M. Le Corbusier's proposals is an over-simplification of the city, whereas what we require is not simplicity, but order.... The modern city is like a large orchestra which often plays an inferior piece of music, and in which the instruments themselves may occasionally be out of tune. It is the business of a reformer to improve the music and the instruments, but not to cut down the range of the orchestra, nor the number of musical effects that are aimed at by it. M. Le Corbusier has not the patience to attempt this, but substitutes for this orchestra a single tin whistle with about five notes, with which he plays a perfectly rhythmical tune. But it is not enough" (Edwards, "The Dead City," p. 137).

CHRONOLOGY OF LE CORBUSIER'S URBAN DESIGNS

Note: The best single source for illustrations of Le Corbusier's designs is in the appropriate volume of the *Œuvre complète* series. See Bibliography.

1887 Born Charles-Édouard Jeanneret at La Chaux-de-Fonds, Switzerland.

1900 Begins study at Art School in La Chaux-de-Fonds.

1906 Travel in Mediterranean region.

1908 Begins working for Auguste Perret in Paris.

1910 Joins Peter Behrens office in Germany.

1920 Together with Ozenfant and Paul Dermée founds magazine *L'Esprit Nouveau*.

1922 Opens studio with cousin Pierre Jeanneret at 35, Rue de Sèvres.
Exhibits A Contemporary City for Three Million People at the Salon d'Automne.

1923 Publishes *Vers une architecture* (*Towards a New Architecture*).

1925 Exhibits the Voisin Plan for Paris at the Salon d'Automne.
Publishes *Urbanisme* (*The City of To-morrow*).
Project for a cité universitaire.
Project for a housing development, Cité Audincourt.
Designs and constructs a housing development at Pessac, near Bordeaux.

1927 Competition project for League of Nations headquarters in Geneva.

1928 Founding member of International Congresses of Modern Architecture (C.I.A.M.).

1929 Visits Latin America. Urbanization studies for Buenos Aires, Montevideo, São Paulo, and Rio de Janeiro.
Redevelopment scheme for the Porte Maillot, Paris.

1930 Becomes a French citizen.
Algiers Project A.
Ville Radieuse Plan.

1932 Master plan for Barcelona.

1933 Plans for Geneva, Stockholm, and Antwerp.
Charter of Athens drawn up at fourth C.I.A.M. Congress.
Algiers Project B.

1934 Algiers Project C.

1934–38 Cooperative village projects.

1934 Plan of Nemours.

1935 Publishes *La ville radieuse* (*The Radiant City*).
Visits the United States.
Plans for Bata community at Hellocourt.

1936 Plan for "l'ilot insalubre" in Paris.
Plan "Paris 37."
Revisits Rio de Janeiro. Assists in planning Ministry of Education building and designs project for University.

1937 Publishes *Quand les cathedrales étaient blanches* (*When the Cathedrals Were White*).

1938 Master plan for Buenos Aires based on 1929 scheme.

1942 Final plan for Algiers.
Founds A.S.C.O.R.A.L. (Assemblée pour une Rénovation Architecturale).

1942–43 Linear-industrial city.

1945–46 Plan for Saint-Gaudens.
Plan for La Rochelle-Pallice.

1946 Assists in planning of United Nations headquarters.
Plan for Saint Dié.

1947	Plans for Marseilles Vieux-Port and Marseilles-Veyre.
	Patents the Modulor.
	Develops the 7 V road system.
	Creates C.I.A.M. grid.
1947–52	Unité d'Habitation at Marseilles.
1948	Plan for Izmir in Turkey.
	Saint Baume and "cité de Sainte-Baume" project.
1949	"Roq et Rob" project for vacation housing at Cap-Martin.
1950	Plan for Bogatá.
1951	Urbanization of Marseilles-Sud.
1951–65	Master plan and monumental architecture of Chandigarh.
1952–53	L'Unité d'Habitation at Nantes.
1956–58	L'Unité d'Habitation at Berlin.
1956–57	Project for Meaux.
1957	L'Unité d'Habitation at Briey-en-Forêt.
1958	Competition design for rebuilding the center of Berlin.
1960	Second project for Meaux.
1965	Dies while swimming off Cap-Martin.

SELECTED BIBLIOGRAPHY

This listing is intended to deal only with Le Corbusier's work in urban design. Some titles, however, include consideration of his other work. Items are listed chronologically by initial publication date. All books are by Le Corbusier unless otherwise specified.

Vers une architecture. Paris: Éditions Crès et Cie, 1923; English translation, *Towards a New Architecture*. New York: Frederick A. Praeger, 1959. Le Corbusier's first major theoretical work. The subject matter deals primarily with architecture, but includes references to urban design.

Urbanisme. Paris: Éditions Crès et Cie, 1925; English translation, *The City of To-morrow*. London: The Architectural Press, 1947. Le Corbusier's first major work on urban design. Contains detailed presentation of A Contemporary City for Three Million People and the Voisin Plan.

Œuvre complète 1910–29, Zurich: Girsberger, 1929; reprinted by George Wittenborn, New York, 1964. Summary of Le Corbusier's complete work between the dates indicated.

Précisions sur un état présent de l'architecture et de l'urbanisme. Paris: Éditions Crès et Cie, 1930; reprinted Éditions Vincent, Fréal et Cie, Paris, 1960. Based on Le Corbusier's South American lectures.

"Twentieth Century Living and Twentieth Century Building," *Decorative Art* (London, *The Studio* yearbook), 1930, pp. 9–20. Le Corbusier summarizes the dominant characteristics of the twentieth century as related to the dwelling.

Adshead, S.D.Z."Camillo Sitte and Le Corbusier," *Town Planning Review*, XIV (November, 1930), 85–94. Sitte's planning principles contrasted with those of Le Corbusier.

La Ville Radieuse. Boulogne (Seine): Éditions de l'Architecture d'Aujourd'hui, 1935; English translation, *The Radiant City*. New York: Grossman, The Orion Press, 1967. Le Corbusier's second major book on urban design. Includes presentation of The Radiant City and other urban projects of the early 1930's.

Œuvre complète 1929–34, Zurich: Girsberger, 1935; reprinted by George Wittenborn, New York, 1964. Summary of Le Corbusier's complete work between the dates indicated.

"What Is America's Problem?" *American Architecture*, CXLVIII (March, 1936), 16–22. Discussion of problems of American cities based on Le Corbusier's observations during his visit to the United States.

Samuel, Godfrey. "Radiant City and Garden Suburb; Le Corbusier's Ville Radieuse," *Royal Institute of British Architects Journal*, XLIII (April 4, 1936), 505–509. Review of *La ville radieuse*, discussing Le Corbusier's ideas with reference to England.

Quand les cathédrales étaient blanches. Paris: Éditions Plon et Cie, 1937; English translation, *When the Cathedrals Were White*. New York: Reynal and Hitchcock, 1947; paperback, New York: McGraw-Hill, 1968. Le Corbusier's commentary on his visit to the United States.

"Module for Recreation," *Architectural Record*, LXXXI (June, 1937), 120–121. A discussion of the time division of the solar day, comparing preindustrial and industrial societies.

Des canons, des munitions? merci! des logis, ... s.v.p. Boulogne (Seine): Éditions de l'Architecture d'Aujourd'hui, 1938.

Œuvre complète 1934–38, Zurich: Girsberger, 1939; reprinted by George Wittenborn, New York, 1964. Summary of Le Corbusier's complete work between the dates indicated.

Le lyrisme des temps nouveaux et l'urbanisme, Strasbourg: Éditions "Le Point," 1939. Issue of an artistic and literary review devoted to Le Corbusier's urban design.

Plan de Buenos Aires. Buenos Aires, 1940. Presentation of a master plan.

Destin de Paris. Paris: Éditions Fernand Sorlot, 1941. Brief summary of Le Corbusier's proposals for Paris.

La Maison des hommes (with François de Pierrefeu). Paris: Éditions Plon et Cie, 1941; reprinted by La Palatine, Paris, 1965. English translation, *The Home of Man*. New York: Frederick A. Praeger, 1948. Generalized presentation of Le Corbusier's urban precepts.

Sur les 4 routes. Paris: Gallimard, 1941; English translation, *The Four Routes*. London: Dennis Dobson Ltd., 1947. Generalized precepts of large-scale planning related to systems of land, water and air transport.

La Charte d'Athens. Paris: Éditions Plon et Cie, 1943; reprinted by Éditions de Minuit, Paris, 1959. Statement of urban design principles based on the 1933 C.I.A.M. Athens Charter.

Les trois établissements humains. Boulogne (Seine): Éditions de l'Architecture d'Aujourd'hui, 1944. A presentation of Le Corbusier's conception of overall land settlement, including the linear-industrial city, the radio-concentric city and the agricultural establishment.

Propos d'urbanisme, Paris: Éditions Bourrelier, 1946; English translation, *Concerning Town Planning*. New Haven: Yale University Press, 1948. Proposals for urban planning in the postwar world, expressed in a series of questions and answers.

"Plans for the Reconstruction of France," *Architectural Record*, XCIX (March, 1946), 92–93. Discusses division of labor between engineer and architect in task of postwar rebuilding.

"Plan for St. Dié," *Architectural Record*, C (October, 1946), 79–83. Discussion of the Saint Dié redevelopment scheme.

Œuvre complète 1938–46. Zurich: Girsberger, 1946; reprinted by George Wittenborn, New York, 1964. Summary of Le Corbusier's complete work between the dates indicated.

Manière de penser sur l'urbanisme, Paris: Éditions de l'Architecture d'Aujourd'hui, 1946; reprinted by Gonthier, Geneva, 1963; English translation, *Manner of Thinking About Urbanism*. New York: McGraw-Hill, 1969. Le Corbusier's general views on planning.

"Architecture and Urbanism," *Progressive Architecture*, XXVIII (February, 1947), 67. Repeats general planning principles and praises Sert and Wiener's Cidade dos Motores in Brazil.

U.N. Headquarters. New York: Reinhold Publishing Corp., 1947. A report by Le Corbusier discussing problems of site selection and design for the U.N. headquarters.

Hellman, Geoffrey. "From Within to Without," *The New Yorker*, XXIII (April 26, 1947), 31–36ff. (May 3, 1947), 36–40ff. General study of Le Corbusier, including his views on urbanism and details of his visits to the United States.

Pokorny, J. and E. Hud. "City Plan for Ziln," *Architectural Record*, CII (August, 1947), 70–71. Postwar plan for Bata manufacturing center in Czechoslovakia based on Le Corbusier's 1935 plan.

New World of Space. New York: Reynal and Hitchcock, 1948. Visual survey based on an exhibition at the Institute of Contemporary Art, Boston, of Le Corbusier's work, with commentary by the architect.

Ghyka, M. "Le Corbusier's Modulor and the Conception of the Golden Mean," *Architectural Review*, CIII (February, 1948), 39–42. Analysis of the mathematical base of the Modulor.

Papadaki, Stamo. *Le Corbusier, Architect, Painter, Writer*. New York: The MacMillan Company, 1948. General presentation of Le Corbusier's work. Includes essays by Joseph Hudnut and others.

Stillman, S. "Comparing Wright and Le Corbusier," *American Institute of Architects Journal*, IX (April–May, 1948), 171–178, 226–233. Frank Lloyd Wright's Broadacre City scheme compared with Le Corbusier's urban conceptions.

Bardi, P. M. *A Critical Review of Le Corbusier*. São Paulo: Museum of Art, 1950. An attempt to analyze Le Corbusier's philosophy, including some reference to his urban design.

Le Modulor. Boulogne (Seine): Éditions de l'Architecture d'Aujourd'hui, 1950; English translation, *The Modulor*. Cambridge: Harvard University Press, 1954; paperback, Cambridge: M.I.T. Press, 1968. Presentation of Le Corbusier's system of proportioning.

L'Unité d'Habitation de Marseilles. Souillac: Éditions "Le Point," 1950; English translation, *The Marseilles Block*. London: Harvill Press, 1953. Presentation of the Marseilles apartment house, relating it to Le Corbusier's general conceptions of urbanism.

"Le Corbusier's Unité d'Habitation," *Architectural Review*, CIX (May, 1951), 292–300. Symposium in which members of the Housing Division, London County Council discuss various aspects of the Marseilles apartment block.

Tyrwhitt, J., J. L. Sert, and E. N. Rogers, *The Heart of the City*. London: Lund Humphries, 1952. Members of C.I.A.M. discuss the urban core. Chapters by Le Corbusier include "The Core as a Meeting Place of the Arts," pp. 41–52, "St. Dié, France," pp. 124–125, "Bogotá, Colombia," pp. 150–152 and "Chandigarh, India," pp. 153–155.

Œuvre complète 1946–52, Zurich: Girsberger, 1953; reprinted by George Wittenborn, New York, 1964. Summary of Le Corbusier's complete work during the dates indicated.

Collins, Peter. "Modulor," *Architectural Review*, CXVI (July, 1954), 5–8. A critical examination of Le Corbusier's Modulor system.

Modulor 2, Paris: Éditions de l'Architecture d'Aujourd'hui, 1955; English translation, *Modulor 2*. Cambridge: Harvard University Press, 1958; paperback, Cambridge: M.I.T.

Press, 1968. Description and applications of Le Corbusier's system of proportioning.

Les Plans Le Corbusier de Paris 1956–1922. Paris: Les Éditions de Minuit, 1956. Principles and examples of urban design. Includes material from *La ville radieuse* and the *Œuvre complète* series.

Stephenson, Gordon. "Le Corbusier," *Royal Architectural Institute of Canada Journal*, XXXIII (June, 1956), 199–203. A paper read before the Vitruvian Society, Toronto. General appreciation of Le Corbusier's character and career.

Boyd, Robin. "The Search for Pleasingness," *Progressive Architecture*, XXXVIII (April, 1957), 193–205. Le Corbusier's Modulor considered in relation to Renaissance proportioning systems.

Mumford, Lewis, "The Sky Line: The Marseilles 'Folly,' " *The New Yorker*, XXXIII (October 5, 1957), 76ff.

Œuvre complète 1952–47, Zurich: Girsberger, 1958, reprinted by George Wittenborn, New York, 1964. Summary of Le Corbusier's complete work between the dates indicated.

L'Urbanisme des trois établissements humains. Paris: Éditions de Minuit, 1959. Le Corbusier's recommendations for a pattern of regional settlement. Incorporates material previously presented in *Les trois établissements humains* (1944).

Blake, Peter. *The Master Builders*. New York: Alfred Knopf, 1960. The life and work of Le Corbusier, Mies van der Rohe, and Frank Lloyd Wright. The portion dealing with Le Corbusier reissued in paperback as *Le Corbusier, Architecture and Form*. Baltimore: Penguin Books, 1963.

Creation is a Patient Search. New York: Frederick A. Praeger, 1960; reprinted, 1966. A selection of Le Corbusier's work, including painting, architecture and urban design, with commentary by the architect.

Le Corbusier 1910–60. New York: George Wittenborn, 1960. Material incorporated from the *Œuvre complète* series covering Le Corbusier's complete work between the dates indicated.

"5 Questions à Le Corbusier," *Zodiac*, VII (1960), 50–55. Le Corbusier answers questions relating to his general philosophy of architecture and urbanism.

"Parlons de Paris," *Zodiac*, VII (1960), 30–37, Reiteration of Paris proposals, together with objections to current suggestions for a "Paris Parallèle."

Columbia University, *Four Great Makers of Modern Architecture*. New York: George Wittenborn, 1963. Record of a symposium devoted to Le Corbusier, Mies van der Rohe, Walter Gropius, and Frank Lloyd Wright. Includes papers on Le Corbusier by José Luis Sert, James Sweeney, Harry Anthony, Rudolph Wittkower, and Ernesto N. Rogers, as well as a convocation address by Le Corbusier.

Metken, G. "Planer von Utopien," *Kunstwerk*, XVII (November, 1963), 13–18. Comparison of Ledoux's visionary urban designs with those of Le Corbusier.

Ragghianti, C. L. "Le Corbusier à Firenze" (with English and French translations), *Zodiac*, XII (1963), 4–17, 219–237. Interpretive study of Le Corbusier's contribution.

Œuvre complète 1957–65. Zurich: Girsberger, 1965; reprinted by George Wittenborn, New York, 1965. Summary of Le Corbusier's complete work between the dates indicated.

Serenyi, Peter. "Le Corbusier's Changing Attitude Toward Form," *Journal of the Society of Architectural Historians*, XXIV (March, 1965), 15–23. Analysis of Le Corbusier's evolution during the 1930's.

Anthony, H. A. "Le Corbusier: His Ideas for Cities," *American Institute of Planners Journal*, XXXII (September, 1966), 279–288. Summarizes Le Corbusier's urban designs and gives brief critical comment.

Evenson, Norma. *Chandigarh*. Berkeley: University of California Press, 1966. A comprehensive study of the planning of Chandigarh, including consideration of both Mayer and Le Corbusier plans. Consult for bibliography of Chandigarh.

Le Corbusier 1910–65, New York: Frederick A. Praeger, 1967. Material reprinted from the *Œuvre complète* series summarizing Le Corbusier's complete work during the period indicated.

Jacobs, A. B. "Observations on Chandigarh," *American Institute of Planners Journal*, XXXIII (January, 1967), 18–26. Summarizes general impressions of city.

Hicks, D. T. "Corb at Pessac," *Architectural Review*, CXLII (September, 1967), 230. Photographs showing the present condition of Le Corbusier's 1925 housing project.

Serenyi, Peter. "Le Corbusier, Fourier and the Monastery at Ema," *Art Bulletin*, XLIX (December, 1967), 277–286. An attempt to analyze Le Corbusier's conception of community structure, relating his ideas to the utopian community of Fourier, and to the monastic ideal.

127

SOURCES OF ILLUSTRATIONS

Norma Evenson: 87, 88, 96, 97, 102

Norma Evenson, *Chandigarh* (Berkeley, University of California Press): 82, 84

Allan B. Jacobs: 86

Journal RAIC-L'IRAC: 75, 76

Richard Langendorf: 81

Le Corbusier, *The City of To-morrow:* 2, 3, 16, 17, 19; *Concerning Town Planning:* 4, 22; *Creation is a Patient Search:* 1, 32, 34, 39, 69, 72; *Manière de Penser sur l'urbanisme:* 55, 56; *Œuvre complète 1910–29:* 5, 6, 7, 8, 9, 10, 11, 12, 13, 14, 15, 18, 21; *Œuvre complète 1929–34:* 37, 45, 46; *Œuvre complète 1934–38:* 30, 31, 38, 40, 51, 52; *Œuvre complète 1938–46:* 25, 50, 53, 57, 59, 60, 61, 62, 64, 65, 68; *Œuvre complète 1946–52:* 58, 63, 66, 67, 70, 73, 74, 77, 83, 88, 89, 90, 91, 92, 93, 98, 99; *Œuvre complète 1952–57:* 85; *Œuvre complète 1957–65:* 23, 78, 79, 94; *Œuvre complète 1910–60:* 54; *Œuvre complète 1910–65:* 35, 80, 100; *The Radiant City:* 20, 24, 26, 27, 28, 29, 33, 36, 41, 42, 43, 44, 47, 48, 49

Rondal Partridge: 95

J. M. Richards, *An Introduction to Modern Architecture* (Baltimore, Penguin Books): 71

Willy Staubli, *Brasilia* (New York, Universe Books): 101